Zen

The Perfect Companion

BLACK DOG
& LEVENTHAL
PUBLISHERS

Published by
Black Dog & Leventhal Publishers, Inc.
151 West 19th Street
New York, NY 10011

Distributed by
Workman Publishing Company
708 Broadway
New York, NY 10003

Manufactured in China

Cover and interior design by Sheila Hart Design
Cover photograph courtesy Corbis
All photographs courtesy Corbis pp. frontispiece, 8, 26, 37, 83, 116, 125, 130, 136,
148, 170, 184, 196, 208, 214, 225, 230, 236, 244, 250, 272, 280
and Getty Images pp. 17, 46, 54, 64, 76, 89, 101, 110, 121, 143, 160, 164, 178, 190, 202, 220, 266

ISBN: 1-57912-279-5

h g f e d c b a

Text and calligraphy copyright © 1992 The Providence Zen Center, Inc.
Adapted from *The Whole World is a Single Flower: 365 Kong-ans for Everyday Life*
with questions and commentary by Zen Master Seung Sahn
first published in 1992 by Charles E. Tuttle Company, Inc.
Adapted by permission of Tuttle Publishing.

Library of Congress Cataloging-in-Publication Data available on file.

Zen means understanding your true self.

"What am I?" That is a very important question: What is the one pure and clear thing? If you find the one pure and clear thing, you will have freedom from life and death. How is it possible to attain freedom from life and death? First, it is necessary that your direction becomes clear; if your direction is clear, then your life is clear. Why do you practice Zen? Why do you eat every day? You must find that!

INTRODUCTION

Put it all down—your opinion, your condition, and your situation. Moment to moment just do it. Then there's no subject, no object, no inside, no outside. Inside and outside already become one. Then your direction and my direction, your action and my action are the same. This is called the Great Bodhisattva Way.

When you put it all down, you can believe in your true self one hundred percent. Then your mind is clear like space, which is clear like a mirror: red comes, red; white comes, white. Someone is hungry, give them food. Someone is thirsty, give them a drink. Everything is reflected in this clear mirror. Then you can see, hear, smell, taste, touch, and think clearly. The sky is blue, the tree is green; salt is salty, sugar is sweet. A dog is barking, "Woof! Woof!" Just like this, everything is truth. So you are also truth.

Then how does this truth function correctly? How do you make your life correct? Moment to moment, you must perceive your correct situation, correct relationship, and correct function. When you are hungry, what? If someone else is hungry, what? If you meet the Buddha, what do you do? Where do you throw away your cigarette ashes? Most people understand all of this, but they cannot actually do it. If you completely do it, then your everyday mind is correct life. Jesus said, "I am the Way, the Truth, and the Life." That is the same point.

Most people understand too much. This understanding cannot help your life. Descartes said, "I think, therefore I am." So "I" makes "I." If you are not thinking, then what? Even if you have a big experience, if you cannot attain the one pure and clear thing, then all your understanding and experience cannot help your practice. Therefore Zen practice is not about understanding. Zen means only go straight, don't know.

Joju once asked Master Nam Cheon, "What is the true way?"

Nam Cheon replied, "Everyday mind is the true way."

"Then should I try to keep it or not?"

Nam Cheon said, "If you try to keep it, you are already mistaken."

"If I do not try to keep it, how can I understand the true way?"

Nam Cheon replied, "The true way is not dependent on understanding or not understanding. Understanding is illusion; not understanding is blankness. If you completely attain the true way of not thinking, it is like space, clear and void. So why do you make right and wrong?" Joju heard that, and got enlightenment.

What did Joju attain?

Often, Zen students want to "keep it." That is just a big mistake. Zen means when you are doing something, just do it. You already know that understanding is illusion. Don't be attached to your understanding! Correct practice means "How does your understanding get digested and become wisdom?" That is true everyday mind.

So why make kong-ans? Since everybody understands too much, we must use understanding medicine. What did Joju attain? If you open your mouth, it's already a mistake. But if you are not thinking, the answer is pure and clear, always in front of you. Then how does your true "I" function correctly and save all beings?

The Tao is called the Great Mother:
empty yet inexhaustible,
it gives birth to infinite worlds.
It is always present within you.
You can use it any way you want.

How does the Tao give birth to infinite worlds? This is the same question, the same point.

In this collection there are Buddhist kong-ans, Christian kong-ans, Taoist kong-ans, and Zen kong-ans. There are old kong-ans, and new kong-ans, but they are all the same: these beautiful words all teach correct direction. If you are attached to beautiful speech or holding your opinion, you cannot attain their true meaning. So put it all down—your opinion, your condition, and your situation. Then your mind is clear like space. Then a correct answer to any kong-an will appear by itself. This is wisdom.

When you try a kong-an, if you don't attain it, don't worry! Don't be attached to the kong-an, and also, don't try to understand the kong-an. Only go straight, don't know: try, try, try for ten thousand years, nonstop. Then you attain the Way, the Truth, and the Life, which means from moment to moment keeping the correct situation, correct relationship, and correct function. That is already Great Love, Great Compassion, and the Great Bodhisattva Way.

Not dependent on words,
A special transmission outside the sutras,
Pointing directly to mind,
See your true nature, become Buddha.

If you wish to pass through this gate, do not give rise to thinking. The Buddha taught all the Dharmas in order to save all minds. When you do not keep any of these minds, then what use is there for Dharmas?

I hope every day you don't make any thing, just do it, from moment to moment, attain the kong-ans, get enlightenment, and save all beings from suffering.

The high sky is always blue. Water always flows into the ocean.

Zen Master Seung Sahn
Providence Zen Center
December, 1991

KONG-ANS

Sok Sahn's "Seven Go Straights"

A long time ago in China, there was a famous Zen Master named Sok Sahn who died without giving transmission. After his funeral ceremony, somebody had to give a formal Dharma speech, so many people asked the Head Monk. As he was about to begin speaking from the high rostrum, Sok Sahn's attendant, a fifteen-year-old boy named Ku Bong, came forward and said, "Our teacher always taught about the seven kinds of going straight:

1. Go straight, resting.
2. Go straight, put it all down.
3. Go straight, the cold, clear water of autumn.
4. Go straight, one mind for 10,000 years.
5. Go straight, cold ashes under a rotten log.
6. Go straight, incense burner in an old temple (very heavy, never moving).
7. Go straight, one line of incense smoke rising in the still air.

If you understand the true meaning of the seven kinds of going straight, then you can give the Dharma speech. If you don't, you cannot."

"One color, different function," the Head Monk replied.

"I cannot believe that."

"If you don't believe me, I'll show you." The Head Monk then lit a stick of incense, placed it in the burner, and quietly watched it burn down. Then he died.

Many people exclaimed, "Ah, this great monk has also died!"

But the attendant only patted the Head Monk's back slowly three times, saying, "Sitting, die. Standing, die. Either way, no hindrance. But Sok Sahn's seven go straights' true meaning cannot be gotten, even in a dream."

1 ⊘ What do Sok Sahn's seven go straights mean?
2 ⊘ "Sitting, die. Standing, die. Either way, no hindrance. But Sok Sahn's seven go straights' meaning cannot be gotten, even in a dream." What does this mean?
3 ⊘ If you were the Head Monk, how would you answer the attendant?

COMMENTARY

Seven doors into the same room. Each door has a different style and function. If you are attached to style and function you cannot enter the room. Only go straight through, take seven steps. Then you can see your true master and say, "How are you today?"

"Fine, and you?" "Very good, thank you." Do you understand that? If you do, then you can pass Sok Sahn's seven go straights.

The Correct Way, Truth and Correct Life

During a Dharma talk at the Lexington Zen Center, Zen Master Seung Sahn said to the assembly, "In the Bible, Jesus says, 'I am the Way, the Truth, and the Life.' Zen also says that if you attain your true self, then you attain the correct way, truth and correct life."

"So what is the correct way?" a student asked Zen Master Seung Sahn.

"Why do you eat every day? Only for your body, because of personal desire? Only for you? That is the same as being an animal. On the other hand, if your eating is for all beings, then your life and direction are clear. The name for that is the correct way."

"Then what is truth?" the student asked.

"If you attain the true way, your mind is clear like space. Then when you see and hear clearly, everything is truth."

"What is correct life?" the student asked.

Zen Master Seung Sahn answered, "If you attain the truth, then you must correctly function as truth, by keeping correct situation, correct relationship, and correct function, moment to moment. The names for this are Great Love, Great Compassion, or the Great Bodhisattva Way. That is correct life."

The student bowed and said, "Thank you very much."

1 ☯ Why do you eat every day?

2 ☯ Why is the sky blue?

3 ☯ When does sugar become sweet?

4 ☯ The way, the truth, and the life—are they the same or different?

COMMENTARY

The student goes to school, the army serves the country, and the teacher works for all students. The dog is barking, "Woof, woof"; the rooster is crowing, "Cock-a-doodle-doo!" Each one understands its job. What is your job? You must remember your obligation to your parents and to your country. When you are hungry, just eat. When someone else is hungry, give them food. Then you attain the correct way, truth, and correct life.

3 Moving Mountain? Moving Boat?

One afternoon, Zen Master Man Gong and several of his students took a boat ride to An Myon Do Island. On the way, he pointed to a mountain and asked his students, "Is the mountain moving or is the boat moving?"

Hae Am stepped forward and said, "Neither the mountain nor the boat is moving. Mind is moving."

"How can you prove that?" Man Gong asked, whereupon Hae Am picked up a handkerchief and waved it. "When did you get this idea?" the Zen Master asked.

1. ☯ Is the mountain moving or is the boat moving?
2. ☯ Zen Master Man Gong asked Hae Am, "When did you get this idea? If you had been there, how would you have answered?
3. ☯ No boat, no mountain. Then what?

COMMENTARY

Mountain is boat, boat is mountain. No mountain, no boat. Mountain is mountain, boat is boat. How do you keep the correct situation, relationship, and function of mountain and boat?

The boat is crossing the ocean to An Myon Do Island. The

ocean is blue, the mountain is also blue. But the ocean is the ocean, and the mountain is the mountain.

Why Do You Have Two Eyes?

During an interview at the Los Angeles Dharma Zen Center, Zen Master Seung Sahn said to a student, "Human beings have two eyes, two nostrils and two ears, but only one mouth." He then asked her:

1. Why do you have two eyes?
2. Why do you have one mouth?
3. Why do you have two ears?

COMMENTARY

Originally, human beings have no eyes, no ears, no nose, no tongue, no body and no mind. Who made the six roots? You, God, Buddha—which one? No, no, no. Cause and effect are very clear. Everything comes from your karma. The British gentleman and Indian laborer hug and pat each other, "Nice to meet you again."

5

How Many Hairs Do You Have on Your Head?

Zen Master Seung Sahn said to the assembly at the Providence Zen Center, "Everyone has hair on their head. Some people have a lot of hair, some people have only a little. Some people have long hair, some people have short hair." Then he asked:

1. ☯ How many hairs do you have on your head?
2. ☯ How long is your hair?

COMMENTARY

The ocean is full of water, there are many clouds in the sky. On the mountain there are numberless trees, and on one head there are many hairs. So form is emptiness, and emptiness is form.

Can you count the hairs on your head? How many do you have? If you find the correct answer then you clearly understand your job.

6

This World Is Complete Stillness

The Lotus Sutra says that all dharmas come from complete stillness. If you just go straight practicing, you have already arrived at Buddha's Hall.

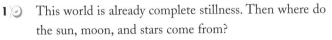

1. This world is already complete stillness. Then where do the sun, moon, and stars come from?
2. What does "just go straight practicing" mean?
3. What is Buddha's Hall?

COMMENTARY

The Bible says God made everything. Buddhism says mind made everything. A sutra says everything comes from emptiness. Which one is correct?

If you are not thinking, there is no name and form. Who made this world of name and form? Do you know? If you don't understand, go drink milk. Then this milk will teach you.

SUMI MOUNTAIN

One day, a monk asked Zen Master Un Mun, "Without thinking, is there a mistake or not?"

"Sumi Mountain," Un Mun replied.

"Already it's without thinking, so why do you add Sumi Mountain?"

"Put it all down."

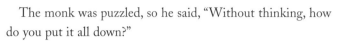

The monk was puzzled, so he said, "Without thinking, how do you put it all down?"

"Then pick it up and carry it away."

1 ◎   Without thinking, is there a mistake or not?

2 ◎   Un Mun said, "Sumi Mountain." What does this mean?

3 ◎   "Put it all down." What does this mean?

4 ◎   "Pick it up and carry it away." What does this mean?

COMMENTARY

A dog is barking, "Woof, woof"; a rooster is crowing, "Cock-a-doodle-doo"; a cat purrs, "Meow, meow." All animals understand their correct speech.

What is your true speech? Open your mouth, and it's already a mistake; close your mouth, it's also a mistake. What can you do? If you remain silent, then Un Mun's stick has already given you thirty blows. What do you say? If you put it all down, then everything is already yours.

8 Shoot Two Geese

During a stay at the Empty Gate Zen Center in Berkeley, Zen Master Seung Sahn told the following story: "One day, a hunter was walking in a field. Suddenly, two geese flew overhead. He reached for an arrow and shot it from his bow. One goose fell. The hunter wanted to shoot again, but he had no more arrows. So he drew his empty bow and shot. The second goose also fell."

1. How do you shoot the empty bow?
2. Why did the second goose fall?

COMMENTARY

One day, a father and his son go for a drive. Their car is hit by a truck. The father is killed, and the son is taken to the hospital. When the son is wheeled into the emergency room, one of the doctors gasps, shouting, "Oh my God, that's my son!" How could that be?

Past Mind, Present Mind, Future Mind Cannot Get Enlightenment

The great Sutra Master Dok Sahn was very famous throughout China for his knowledge of the Diamond Sutra. For years he always carried it wherever he went, stopping at temples and lecture halls throughout the country. One day, he learned that there was a temple in the South where the monks did nothing all day but sit facing the wall and sleep, and they still got enlightenment. "That's crazy," Dok Sahn thought. "They don't understand Buddha's teaching, Buddha's actions, or Buddha's mind. How can they get enlightenment? I'll go hit them, wake them up, and teach them the way of the sutras."

So, he walked south several hundred miles. One afternoon, he decided to rest for a little while at a small tea house. It was past lunch time, and he was very hungry. The owner, an old woman, was honored to have such a great monk stop at her tea house. She bowed to him and said, "Good afternoon, great monk! Where are you coming from?"

"From the North."

"Where are you going?"

"South."

Zen

"Why are you going south?"

"I am a Diamond Sutra Master," Dok Sahn replied. "At a temple in the South, the monks only sit facing the wall, sleep, and still get enlightenment. That's crazy! So I will go hit them, wake them up and teach them the Diamond Sutra."

"Oh, that's wonderful!" the woman said. "You are a Diamond Sutra Master! Well, I have a question for you. If you answer correctly, your lunch is free. But if you are wrong, I cannot serve you any lunch."

Dok Sahn grew very angry at this. "Shut up! You are speaking to a Diamond Sutra Master! My knowledge of it is unparalleled throughout the land! Ask me anything!"

"Good," the woman said. "Now, the Diamond Sutra says, 'Past mind cannot get enlightenment, present mind cannot get enlightenment, and future mind cannot get enlightenment.' So I ask you, with what kind of mind will you eat lunch?"

Dok Sahn's jaw dropped. He stammered but could not answer and his face turned red. He was completely stuck. The old woman said, "You've studied the great Diamond Sutra for ten years! If you cannot answer this question, how will you teach the sleeping monks of the South?"

1 ⊘ This world is complete stillness. Where do north and south come from?

2 ⊘ What is mind?

3 ⊘ The woman asked, "Past mind cannot get enlightenment, present mind cannot get enlightenment, and future mind cannot get enlightenment. With what kind of mind will you eat lunch?" If you were Dok Sahn, what could you do?

COMMENTARY

Silence is better than holiness, so one action is better than all the sutras. If you are attached to words and speech, you won't understand a melon's taste; you will only understand its outside form. If you want to understand a melon's taste, then cut a piece and put it in your mouth. A melon grows and ripens by itself; it never explains to human beings its situation and condition.

If you are attached to the sutras, you only understand Buddha's speech. If you want to attain Buddha's mind, then from moment to moment put down your opinion, condition, and situation. Only help all beings. Then Buddha appears in front of you. This is enlightenment and freedom from life and death.

10 The Old Woman Burns the Hermitage

It is said that if you practice hard for ten years you will attain something. So, as is customary among many Buddhist laypeople, an old woman in China once supported a monk for ten years. She provided him with food and clothing, and allowed him to live in a hermitage that she provided. For his part, the monk only practiced very, very hard, and did not have to concern himself with anything else.

After ten years, however, there was still no news from the monk. "What did he attain?" she wondered. "I must test this monk." So one afternoon, the woman summoned her sixteen-year-old daughter, who was considered one of the most beautiful girls in the village. Her mother asked her to put on makeup, her best perfume, and clothing made of the finest materials. Then she gave her daughter instructions for testing the monk, loaded her up with plenty of fine food and clothing, and sent her off to the hermitage. The woman's daughter was very excited about the plan!

When she arrived at the hermitage, she bowed to the monk and said, "You have been here for ten years, so my mother made this special food and clothing for you."

"Oh, thank you very much," the monk replied. "Your mother is a great Bodhisattva for supporting me like this for so long."

Just then, the girl strongly embraced the monk, kissed him, and said, "How do you feel now?"

"Rotten log on cold rocks. No warmth in winter."

Releasing him, the girl bowed deeply and said, "You are certainly a great monk!" She returned home, full of happiness and admiration, to report the incident to her mother. "Mother, Mother! This monk's center is very strong, his mind is not moving! He must have attained something!"

"It doesn't matter if his center is strong, or if his mind cannot be moved, or if he is a wonderful monk. What I want to know is what did he say?"

"Oh, his words were also wonderful, Mother. He said, 'Rotten log on cold rocks. No warmth in winter.'"

"What!?" the old woman shouted. Fuming, she grabbed a big stick, ran to the hermitage and mercilessly beat the monk, shouting, "Go away! Get out of here! I've spent ten years helping a demon!" Then she burned the hermitage to the ground.

1 ◯ What kind of practice did this monk do for ten years?

2 ◯ The girl strongly embraced the monk and said, "How do

you feel now?" If you were the monk, what could you do?

3 Where is the monk's mistake?

4 What did the old woman attain that made her beat the monk?

5 If you were the old woman and the monk said, "Rotten log on cold rocks. No warmth in winter," what kind of teaching could you give him?

COMMENTARY

Mother has mother's job, daughter has daughter's job, businessman has businessman's job, monk has monk's job. If you don't understand your job, you don't understand your responsibility.

The monk sat for ten years. What is his job? If you are holding something, and attached to something, then you lose your original job. Put it all down, then your original job and your correct situation, correct relationship, and correct function will appear clearly.

If you understand one, you lose everything. If you attain one, then you get everything. Be careful! What are you doing now? Just do it.

Why Do You Have Five Fingers?

During a Dharma talk at the Cambridge Zen Center, Zen Master Seung Sahn said to the assembly, "Human beings have one head, two arms, one body, and two legs." Then he asked:

1 ⊙   Why do you have five fingers?

2 ⊙   Why do you have two legs?

Commentary

Originally, there are no eyes, no ears, no nose, no tongue, no body, and no mind, which means originally no color, no sound, no smell, no taste, no touch, and no object of mind. Mind appears, everything appears. Mind disappears, and everything disappears. When mind is clear, everything is clear, and when mind is not clear, everything is not clear.

See clearly, hear clearly, think clearly. Don't be attached to name and form. If your mind is clear like space then everything is reflected: the sky is blue, the tree is green, the dog is barking, "Woof, woof." This is truth. If you attain the function of truth, that is correct life: If someone is hungry, give them food; if someone is thirsty, give them a drink.

12

How Do You Get Out of the Net?

One day, Zen Master Man Gong sat on the high rostrum and gave the Hae Jae Dharma speech to mark the end of the three-month winter Kyol Che. "All of you sat in the Dharma Room for three months. That is very, very wonderful. As for me, I only stayed in my room making a net. This net is made from a special string. It is very strong and can catch Buddha, Dharma, Bodhisattvas, human beings—everything. How do you get out of this net?"

Some students shouted, "KATZ!" Others hit the floor, or raised a fist, or said, "The sky is blue, the tree is green." One said, "Already got out. How are you, great Zen Master?" while another shouted from the back of the room, "Don't make net!"

Many answers were given, but to each Man Gong only responded, "Aha! I've caught a big fish!"

1   How do you get out of Zen Master Man Gong's net?

COMMENTARY

Don't make anything. If you make something, then something is a hindrance. The sky is always bright. Clouds appear and the sky is dark. The wind blows and the clouds disappear. When you put down your opinions and conditions, the correct situation,

correct relationship and correct function will appear. If you are attached to speech and words then you are already dead. Be careful.

Understand that to return to primary point, you must begin at 0°, go around the circle, and return to 360°.*

13

NO HINDRANCE

One day, a nun visited Zen Master Song Sahn, "What is Dharma?" she asked.

"No hindrance."

"Then what does 'no hindrance' mean?"

Song Sahn replied, "Why do you wear clothes?"

At this, the nun stripped naked and walked to the door.

1 ☯ What is Dharma?

2 ☯ If you were Zen Master Song Sahn, at that time what would you do?

3 ☯ The nun stripped naked. Is that no hindrance?

COMMENTARY

A tree understands tree's job, and water understands water's

---

* For an explanation of the Zen Circle, see kong-an #37, "The Zen Circle."

job. What is a Zen Master's job? What is a nun's correct job? If you are attached to speech you will go to hell like an arrow. If you digest speech you can kill all Buddhas and Bodhisattvas. Which one do you like? Put it all down. Go to the store and drink iced tea.

Where Does the Bell Sound Come From?

One day, as the big temple bell was being rung, the Buddha asked Ananda, "Where does the bell sound come from?"

"The bell."

The Buddha said, "The bell? But if there were no bell stick, how would the sound appear?"

Ananda hastily corrected himself. "The stick! The stick!"

"The stick? If there were no air, how could the sound come here?"

"Yes! Of course! It comes from the air!"

The Buddha asked, "Air? But unless you have an ear, you cannot hear the bell sound."

"Yes! I need an ear to hear it. So it comes from my ear."

The Buddha replied, "Your ear? If you have no consciousness, how can you understand the bell sound?"

"My consciousness makes the sound."

"Your consciousness? So, Ananda, if you have no mind, how do you hear the bell sound?"

"It was created by mind alone."

1 🕑 Everything is created by mind alone. Is that correct?

2 🕑 If you have no mind, where does the bell sound go?

3 🕑 Where does the bell sound come from?

COMMENTARY

True form is without thinking. Truth is unmoving. Name and form, appearing and disappearing—these things never existed. Time and space are always moving. The world of name is the world of opposites. See, hear, smell, speak, act, and think clearly.

BRING THIS SOUND HERE

Many students visited Zen Master Kyong Bong at the Absolute Bliss Zen Center in Tong Do Sah Temple. After they bowed to the Zen Master, he would always ask, "How are you?"

One student responded, "Fine. And you?"

Kyong Bong said, "Give me your hand."

Then he held the student's hand, palm up, slapped it and said, "Catch this sound and bring it to me."

1 ☺ If you were the student, how could you catch this sound and bring it to the Zen Master?

2 ☺ The Hua Yen Sutra says, "All things created by mind alone." Then is this sound created by mind as well?

Commentary

The spring wind brings flowers, summer wind brings rain, autumn wind brings fruit, and winter wind brings snow. If you want the sound to become yours, then speech and words cannot help you. If you are attached to speech and words, that's already a big mistake.

How Many Steps Did You Take to Get Here?

A monk visited Zen Master Kyong Bong and asked, "What is Truth?"

"Where are you coming from?"

春來草自青

16

"Pusan."

"Oh, that's very far away," Kyong Bong replied. "How many steps did you take to get here?"

1 ⊘ If you were the monk, how would you answer?

COMMENTARY

East wind blowing, cloud goes west; south wind blowing, cloud goes north. Rounding a corner, the bus honks its horn, "Beep, beep." What can you do? You already understand. But be careful of the fish hook. Enough-mind fish never touches the hook. Swimming in the ocean means freedom everywhere.

17

HOW DO YOU CLEAN YOUR MIND?

Diamond Mountain is a famous mountain in Korea. Near the summit, there was an old Zen center named Maha Yon, and at the bottom was a sutra temple named Yu Jom Sah, where nearly 500 monks studied sutras. Halfway up the mountain, between Maha Yon and Yu Jom Sah, was the famous Diamond Mountain Hot Spring. The owner of the hot spring was a Buddhist laywoman who always let monks in, free of charge.

One day a famous sutra master from Yu Jom Sah, named Sol

Hae, came to use the hot spring. After he finished bathing, he complimented the owner, "Oh, thank you very much. Excellent springs! Your hot tub is the best in the world."

"You're welcome," the owner replied. "Your face looks very wonderful! Now, I have a question for you: You cleaned your body in the hot tub. How do you clean your mind?"

Sol Hae was stuck, and could not answer.

1 ⊘   What is mind?

2 ⊘   Body and mind—are they the same or different?

3 ⊘   If you were the great sutra master, how would you answer?

COMMENTARY

The Sixth Patriarch said that originally there is nothing. So if you make something, you hinder something. If you want to understand the realm of the Buddhas then keep a mind which is clear like space. Then, your mind is like a clear mirror: red comes, red is reflected; white comes, white. Anything coming and going is no hindrance. If you have mind, you must clean it. If you have no mind, cleaning is not necessary. Put it down—that will help your life.

18

Great Teacher Bu Dae Sa Expounds the Diamond Sutra

Emporer Yang Mu Je requested Great Teacher Bu Dae Sa to expound the Diamond Sutra. The Great Teacher climbed onto the high rostrum, shook the desk once, and then got down off the seat. Emperor Yang Mu Je was astonished. Master Jo Gang asked him, "Does your majesty understand?"

The Emperor said, "No, I do not understand."

"The Great Teacher Bu Dae Sa has finished expounding the sutra," Master Ji Gang said.

1. Why did the Great Teacher Bu Dae Sa shake his desk once?

2. Emperor Yang Mu Je said, "I don't understand." What does this mean?

3. Master Ji Gang said, "The Great Teacher Bu Dae Sa has finished expounding the sutra." What does this mean?

COMMENTARY

Do you see? Do you hear? The sun, the moon, the stars, the trees, and the rivers are already teaching us the Diamond Sutra. If you open your mouth, you lose the Diamond Sutra's true meaning. Just seeing, just hearing, just smelling is better than the Diamond Sutra. The rooster crows, "Cock-a-doodle-doo." The dog barks, "Woof, woof." Is that the Diamond Sutra or not? Don't check, put it down. What are you doing now? Just do it.

How Do You Clean Dust?

A renowned Dharma Master from Hong Kong named Sae Jin once gave a Dharma talk at the New York Zen Center. After the talk, he asked for questions. People raised many interesting questions about his talk, to which he gave insightful answers. Finally, one student asked him, "Your name is 'Sae Jin,' which means 'Clean Dust,' but the Sixth Patriarch said, 'Originally nothing. Where is dust?' So, how can you clean dust?"

Sae Jin was stuck. Although his understanding was great, he only understood the sutras, but did not understand Zen, so he couldn't say anything.

1 ⊘ The Sixth Patriarch said, "Originally nothing." What does this mean?

2 ⊘ The student asked, "Your name is 'Sae Jin,' which means 'Clean Dust.' … How can you clean dust?" If you were Sae Jin, what could you do?

The Sixth Patriarch wrote a poem:

> *Bodhi has no tree.*
> *Clear mirror has no stand.*
> *Originally nothing.*
> *Where is dust?*

So originally there is nothing. Where does Bodhi come from? Where does the clear mirror come from? If you are originally nothing, how can you even say, "Originally nothing? Where is dust?" That is a big mistake. If you attain the Sixth Patriarch's mistake then you attain his true meaning, and these questions are no hindrance. But you must hit the Sixth Patriarch's mistake. That is very necessary.

Don't Attach to Anything

A long time ago in China, before he became the Sixth Patriarch, Layman No worked in the mountains every day, gathering firewood to sell in the city. He would use the money he made to buy food, clothing, and whatever else was needed to help his mother. He worked only to support her.

One afternoon, on his way back from town, he came upon a monk who was reciting the Diamond Sutra. Layman No stood still and quietly listened, hearing the line, "Don't Attach to Anything Which Arises in the Mind." At this, he suddenly got the Great Enlightenment.

1.   "Don't Attach to Anything Which Arises in the Mind." What does this mean?
2.   What did he attain?
3.   What is the Great Enlightenment?

COMMENTARY

If you have no "I-me-my," then moment-to-moment, keeping correct situation, correct relationship, and correct function is possible. If you are holding something or attached to something, when you die you will go straight to hell. Layman No worked every day only for his mother. He heard one word and understood himself. If you don't hold anything, you can also attain your true self and freedom from life and death. That is very, very wonderful!

See True Buddha

The Diamond Sutra says, "All formations are impermanent.
If you view all appearances as non-appearance, then you can
see true Buddha."

But everything is impermanent, so Buddha is impermanent, and you are also impermanent. How can impermanence
see impermanence? Therefore, the sentence in the Diamond
Sutra should be changed to "If you view all appearance as
non-appearance, this view is Buddha."

1. How do you view all appearance as non-appearance?
2. What is "true Buddha"?
3. "This view is Buddha." What does this mean?

Commentary

Before you are born, there are no six roots, six consciousnesses, or six dusts. After you are born, these six roots, consciousnesses, and dusts control you. This is suffering. If you
control them, then nothing is a hindrance: you are already
beyond life and death. Moment to moment, only help all
beings. This is the great Bodhisattva Way.

This Stillness Is Bliss

The Mahaparinirvana Sutra says, "All things are appearing and disappearing. That is the law of appearing and disappearing. When both appearing and disappearing disappear, this stillness is bliss."

All human beings have two bodies: a form-body and a Dharma-body. The form-body is always appearing and disappearing, so it is always suffering and therefore it cannot attain true bliss. The Dharma-body never appears or disappears, so it has no form, feelings, perceptions, impulses, or consciousness. It is like the rocks and the trees; therefore it, too, cannot get bliss.

1. ⊘ What is the law of appearing and disappearing?
2. ⊘ How do "both appearing and disappearing disappear"?
3. ⊘ Are the form-body and the Dharma-body the same or different?
4. ⊘ What kind of body gets "stillness is bliss"?

COMMENTARY

A long time ago in China, there was a Sutra Master named Ji Do who studied the Mahaparinirvana Sutra for ten years. He understood that the form-body cannot get bliss because it s always appearing and disappearing, but he still could not understand how the Dharma-body gets bliss, since it has no feelings and is like the rocks and trees. So Ji Do had a big question: "How does the Dharma-body get bliss?"

In order to find an explanation, he visited the Sixth Patriarch. The Sixth Patriarch asked him, "Is it your form-body or Dharma-body which is asking this question? If it is your form-body, then you appear and disappear; if it is your Dharma-body, you are like the rocks and the trees, and you cannot hear my speech. What do you say?" Ji Do was completely stuck. Then the Sixth Patriarch said, "Don't make anything!" Ji Do heard this and was instantly enlightened.

Is Your Body Form or Emptiness?

The Heart Sutra says, "Avalokiteshvara Bodhisattva perceives that all five *skandhas* are empty." So form is emptiness, emptiness is form. Originally, there are no eyes, no ears, no nose, no tongue, no body, and no mind.

1 ⊘ Is your body a form or emptiness?
2 ⊘ "All five skandhas are empty." What does this mean?

COMMENTARY

One mind appears and the whole universe appears. One mind disappears and the whole universe disappears. The clouds float from the ocean, rain falls from the sky.

But if one mind never appears or disappears, then what? What do you see now? What do you hear now? Your mind is like a clear mirror. The mountain is blue, water is flowing.

24

What Is Insight?

There are three kinds of practice in Therevada Buddhism:

Sila – Precepts

Samadhi – Meditation

Prajna – Wisdom

If you practice these three things, you get insight into impermanence, insight into impurity and insight into non-self.

1 ☺ What is insight into impermanence?

2 ☺ What is insight into impurity?

3 ☺ What is insight into non-self?

4 ☺ There are three kinds of insight. Are they the same or different?

⊙ When you see the mountain and the river, what kind of insight is this?

Commentary

The dog is barking, "Woof, woof"; the rooster is crowing, "Cock-a-doodle-doo!" Are these coming or going? Are they inside or outside your mind, pure or impure? Don't make anything! If you make something, you lose your life. Without making anything, you are already complete.

Nirvana and Annutara Samyak Sambodhi

The Heart Sutra says that there is no cognition, and no attainment with nothing to attain. Next, it says, "The Boddhisatva depends on Prajna Paramita and … dwells in Nirvana." Finally, it says, "In the three worlds all Buddhas depend on Prajna Paramita and attain Annutara Samyak Sambodhi."

1 ⊙ What is Nirvana?
2 ⊙ What is Annutara Samyak Sambodhi?
3 ⊙ If there is "No cognition and no attainment with

nothing to attain," how do all Buddhas attain
Annutara Samyak Sambodhi?

4 "The Bodhisattva depends on Prajna Paramita and …
dwells in Nirvana." "All Buddhas depend on Prajna
Paramita and attain Annutara Samyak Sambodhi." If
you depend on Prajna Paramita, what do you get?

5 What do you depend on?

COMMENTARY

"Form is emptiness. Emptiness is form." This is the world
of opposites. "No form. No emptiness." This is Nirvana, the
absolute world. "Form is form. Emptiness is emptiness." This
is Annutara Samyak Sambodhi, or the complete world.

Are these three the same or different? If you don't understand,
then you must find some meat and give it to a hungry dog. This
dog will teach you the true meaning of the Heart Sutra.

All Things Are Created by Mind Alone

The Hua Yen (Avatamuska) Sutra says, "If you wish to thoroughly understand all Buddhas of the past, present, and future,

Zen

55

then you should view the nature of the whole universe as being created by mind alone."

1. Are there differences between past, present, and future Buddhas?
2. What is "the nature of the whole universe"?
3. Mind created everything. What created mind?

COMMENTARY

A long time ago in Korea, a famous Sutra Master named Dae Oh Sunim traveled to Hae In Sah Temple to lecture on the Hua Yen Sutra. He concluded his week's teaching by stating, "For forty-nine years, the Buddha taught only one word: 'All things are created by mind alone.'"

After the talk, there were many questions and answers. Then one young Zen monk stood up and asked, "You said that all things are created by mind alone. My question is: where does this mind come from?" Dae Oh Sunim was completely stuck, and could not answer.

Do you understand? If not, go ask a tree. The tree will answer for you.

The Stone Man Is Crying

As a young monk, Zen Master Man Gong was asked, "The ten thousand dharmas return to the One. Where does the One return?" He could not answer this question, and for a long time it would not let him go. Then one day, he heard the sound of the temple bell, and got enlightenment. Overjoyed, and very confident, he went around from temple to temple and met with many Sutra Masters. He asked one of them, "The Lotus Sutra talks about the Dharma. Where does the Dharma come from?" The Sutra Master could not answer. Man Gong hit him and said, "That is Dharma. You should understand that."

He asked another temple's Sutra Master, "The Hua Yen Sutra talks about mind. What is mind?" The Sutra Master could not answer him, so Man Gong hit him, too.

He went all around hitting many Sutra Masters. Man Gong had too much pride, thinking, "I already got enlightenment." Eventually he met Zen Master Kyong Ho at Ma Gok Sah Temple. "Man Gong Sunim, I heard you got enlightenment," the famous Master said.

"Yes, I did."

"Then I have something to ask you. This is a brush. This is

paper. Are they the same or different?"

Man Gong thought, "That's no problem, very easy," and replied, "The paper is the brush, and the brush is the paper."

"Then I ask you: The paper and the brush come from where?"

Man Gong shouted, "KATZ!"

"Not good, not bad," Kyong Ho said, and asked several more questions, which Man Gong answered easily. Finally, Kyong Ho asked, "The traditional funeral ceremony chant says, 'The stone man is crying.' What does this mean?"

Man Gong was stuck. He had never heard this kind of question before. His mind became tight, and all his pride vanished. Kyong Ho shouted at him, "You don't understand this meaning! How can you say, 'The brush is the paper, the paper is the brush'?"

Man Gong bowed deeply and said, "I'm sorry. Please teach me."

"A long time ago, a monk asked Zen Master Joju, 'Does a dog have Buddha nature?' Joju said, 'Mu.' Do you understand that?"

"I don't know."

Then Kyong Ho said, "Only go straight, don't know! OK?"

For the next three years, Man Gong did very hard training, always keeping only don't-know. One day, he was sitting at Tong Do Sah's Absolute Bliss Zen Center. Again, he heard the sound of a bell and this time got complete enlightenment. He sent a letter to Kyong Ho that said, "Thank you very much for your great teaching. Now I understand: kimchee is hot, sugar is sweet."

Zen Master Kyong Ho was very happy, and gave Dharma Transmission to Man Gong.

1 ☉ Brush and paper: are they the same or different?

2 ☉ Man Gong shouted, "KATZ!" What does this mean?

3 ☉ "The stone man is crying." What does this mean?

4 ☉ Man Gong first heard the bell and got his enlightenment. Later, he heard the bell and again got enlightenment. His first enlightenment and his second enlightenment—how are they different?

5 ☉ "Kimchee is hot, sugar is sweet." What does this mean?

COMMENTARY

$1 + 2 = 3$. $3 \times 0 = 0$. $3 \times 3 = 9$. Are these the same or different? If you say the same, you don't understand mathematics. If you say different, you also don't understand mathematics. $10,000 \times 0 = 0$. Mountain $\times$ 0 = 0. Water $\times$ 0 = 0. Is that correct? But what is mountain $\times$ mountain? What is water $\times$ water? It's very clear— the correct answer already appears.

Where is Man Gong's first mistake? When did Man Gong

completely attain? You already understand. When standing in front of the Buddha, if you hear the sound of the moktak, just bow. That is your original face.

Three Statements

The Compass of Zen says that there are three kinds of Zen:

Theoretical Zen teaches, "Form is emptiness. Emptiness is form."

Tathgata Zen teaches, "No form. No emptiness."

Patriarchal Zen teaches, "Form is form. Emptiness is emptiness."

1 ⊘ Which one is correct?

2 ⊘ "Form is emptiness. Emptiness is form." What does this mean?

3 ⊘ "No form. No emptiness." What does this mean?

4 ⊘ "Form is form. Emptiness is emptiness." What does this mean?

COMMENTARY

Mountain is water, water is mountain. But originally there is nothing. If you don't make anything, then no mountain and no water. Then your mind is clear like space, which means it is clear like a mirror: mountain is mountain, water is water. The mirror correctly reflects everything.

Of these three statements, which one is correct? If you find the correct one, you lose your life; if you cannot find it, you lose your body. What can you do? Go drink tea—then it's clearly in front of you: mountain is blue, water is flowing.

Not Depending on Anything

Not depending on words, a special transmission outside the sutras, pointing directly to mind: see your true nature, become Buddha.

1. What is "a special transmission outside the sutras"?
2. How do you point directly to mind?
3. "See your true nature, become Buddha." What does this mean?

COMMENTARY

This world was originally complete stillness. If mind appears, then the sky, the earth, the mountains, the rivers, everything appears. If mind disappears, where do these things return to? If you say, "They return to emptiness," then you have opened your mouth, which is already a mistake. What can you do? If you don't understand, go to the kitchen and drink cold water.

30

What Do You Need?

The Buddha taught all the Dharmas in order to save all minds. When you do not keep all these minds, what use is there for the Dharmas?

1. How do you not keep all these minds?
2. What use is there for the Dharmas?
3. Is mind first or Dharma first?
4. No Dharma, no mind. Then what?

COMMENTARY

Mind appears, Dharma appears. Dharma appears—like, dislike, coming, going, life and death—all these things appear.

When mind disappears, then everything disappears, speech and words also disappear. Opening your mouth is a big mistake. What can you do? Put it all down. Don't touch the fish hook. When you are hungry, just eat. When you are thirsty, just drink.

Three Occasions of the Buddha's Transmission to Mahakashyapa

One morning, the Buddha sat in front of the Pagoda of Many Children. Many disciples had gathered from near and far to hear his Dharma speech. Everyone waited for him to begin, but the Buddha did not open his mouth. In the front rows were the older students, including many venerable monks. The new monks and novices sat far away in the back. Mahakashyapa arrived and walked to the front, in front of the Buddha. Though he was an old man, he had only recently become a monk, so everyone thought it was incorrect of him to walk in front of the Buddha. But when the Buddha saw him, he moved over and allowed Mahakashyapa to sit next to him on his cushion. Everyone was surprised and amazed. By this action, the Buddha was demonstrating the equality of dharma nature.

1 The Buddha was at Vulture's Peak. Over a thousand disciples were assembled to hear him speak, but he did not

31

迦
葉
破
顔

open his mouth. After several minutes of silence, he held up a flower before the assembly. No one understood. Only Mahakashyapa smiled. Then the Buddha said, "I transmit my true Dharma to you."

111 The Buddha died when he was eighty years old. In those days, people often lived to one hundred, so many of his disciples did a lot of checking: "Why did the Buddha die?" "Why didn't he live longer?" "This is not fair." Furthermore, they could not begin the funeral ceremony without the Buddha's great disciple, Mahakashyapa. They anxiously waited seven days, when finally Mahakashyapa arrived. The wood was stacked high for the funeral pyre and on top was the gold coffin containing the Buddha's body. Perceiving that everyone was still sad and confused, Mahakashyapa bowed three times in front of the pyre, walked clockwise around it three times, and bowed in front of it three times.

After the last bow, there was a big clap of thunder. The coffin broke open and the Buddha's feet appeared. Everyone was very shocked and instantly realized this teaching:

Only the Buddha's body had died, but the true Buddha never dies.

Ia 🕖 Mahakashyapa sat next to the Buddha. What does this mean?

b 🕖 What is the equality of dharma nature?

IIa 🕖 Why did Mahakashyapa smile?

b 🕖 What kind of Dharma was transmitted to him?

IIIa 🕖 The Buddha's feet broke through the coffin. What does this mean?

b 🕖 "Only the Buddha's body had died, but the true Buddha never dies." What does this mean?

COMMENTARY

The Buddha and Mahakashyapa are good actors. But nobody understands their meaning: Only the Buddha and Mahakashyapa understand each other, so they are not good actors. If you have neither the Buddha nor Mahakashyapa, then everything is clear: the sky is blue, the tree is green, water is flowing. You can see clearly.

But the Buddha and Mahakashyapa take away all of their students' eyes, ears, noses, and mouths. This is a number one bad job. If you attain this "bad job" then you are better than the Buddha and Mahakashyapa. How wonderful!

Pointing Directly to Mind

A long time ago in China, Zen Master Dong Sahn was asked, "What is Buddha?" He answered, "Three pounds of flax." When someone asked Zen Master Un Mun the same question, he replied, "Dry shit on a stick," and when Zen Master Joju was asked, "Why did Bodhidharma come to China?" he answered, "The cypress tree in the garden."

1. ⊙ "What is Buddha?" Zen Master Dong Sahn answered, "Three pounds of flax." That is only 80 percent correct. What is 100 percent?

2. ⊙ "What is Buddha?" Zen Master Un Mun answered, "Dry shit on a stick." That was a big mistake. Where is the mistake?

3. ⊙ When the Zen Master Joju was asked, "Why did Bodhidharma come to China?" he answered, "The cypress tree in the garden." That was not correct. How can you make it correct?

Commentary

If you are attached to speech, then you lose your life. If you perceive speech then you understand correct situation. If you understand the correct function of speech, then you will get complete freedom from life and death. Ice becomes water, water becomes steam. So, ice, water, and steam—are they the same or different? If you say "the same" you lose your mouth. If you say "different" your mouth goes to hell. What can you do? Hear clearly, smell clearly, think clearly—then you will attain the truth and the correct way. Be careful of your ears. If you are attached to speech, you will go to hell like an arrow.

33

See True Nature, Become Buddha

1. The willow is green, the flowers are red. Is that nature or is that Buddha?

2. The crow is black, the crane is white. Do you see Buddha? Do you hear nature?

COMMENTARY

The Diamond Sutra says that all formations are always appearing and disappearing. If you view all appearances as non-appearances, then you can see Buddha. If you want to see Buddha, Buddha has already disappeared. If you don't want to see Buddha, then seeing, hearing, smelling, touching, tast-

ing—everything is Buddha. The flower is red, the tree is
green, the sky is blue. You and these things are never separate.
Then you are Buddha.

Great Enlightenment

Heaven earth, earth heaven, heaven earth revolve.
Water mountain, mountain water, water mountain emptiness.
Heaven heaven, earth earth, when did they ever revolve?
Mountain mountain, water water, each is separate from the other.

There are three kinds of enlightenment. First Enlightenment
means "Primary Point." Original Enlightenment is "Like-This,"
which means truth. Final Enlightenment is "Just-Like-This,"
which means correct function is correct life.

1. What is "Primary Point"?
2. What does "Like-This" mean?
3. What does "Just-Like-This" mean?
4. Of the four lines in the poem above, which one is
   Great Enlightenment?

COMMENTARY

In the spring, the fog is so dense you cannot see through it. In the summer, there is much rain. In the fall, many clouds come and go quickly. In the winter, snow falls everywhere. Fog, rain, clouds, and snow—are they the same or different? Where do they come from? If you say they are the same, you have already lost your tongue. If you say they are different, you lose your body. What can you do? 1 + 2 = 3, 3 x 3 = 9, but 9 x 0 = 0. If you attain that number then your true face is in front of you. How wonderful!

35

The Three Essential Elements of Zen

There are three essential elements of Zen:

Great Faith

Great Courage

Great Question

If you have Great Faith, you attain the correct way.

If you have Great Courage, you attain truth.

If you have Great Question, you attain the correct life.

Having Great Faith is like a hen sitting on her eggs to keep hem warm. She always keeps her direction, never moving, no matter what.

Having Great Courage is like a cat catching a mouse. The cat focuses one hundred percent of its strength and attention on one point and one action: first on waiting, then on pouncing.

Having Great Question is like a person who has not eaten in three days, who only thinks of food. Or it is like someone who is thirsty, having worked all day in the hot sun with nothing to drink, and who thinks only of water. Or is it like a child whose mother is far away: this child wants his mother, and his mind thinks only of her. Great Question is single-mindedness, a mind that is focused on only one thing.

1 ⊙   What is Great Faith?

2 ⊙   What is Great Courage?

3 ⊙   What is Great Question?

COMMENTARY

One, two, three. Where do these numbers come from? You already understand. Children want candy; business-people want money; scholars want to become famous. There are many kinds of people and many directions. Where do they finally go? If you attain this point, you attain human nature and universal substance. If you attain universal substance, you can see and hear clearly, and your emotions, will, and wisdom can function correctly. Then your life is correct and you can help all beings. This is called the Great Bodhisattva Way.

36

ENERGY IN ZEN

When walking, standing, sitting, lying down, speaking, being silent, moving, being still, at all times, in all places, without interruption, what is this?

One mind is infinite kalpas.

1. "All times" and "all places" come from where?
2. "One mind is infinite kalpas." Are infinite kalpas inside or outside this one mind?
3. What is one mind?
4. What are "infinite kalpas"?

COMMENTARY

The Avatamsaka Sutra says, "If you wish to thoroughly understand all the Buddhas of the past, present, and future, then you should view the nature of the whole universe as being created by mind alone." If you have no mind, where can the Buddha stay? Who comes? Who goes? If "one mind" disappears, where are time and space? Put it down, then everything is clear. The mountain is blue, water is flowing.

The Zen Circle

We sometimes explain Zen by means of a circle. The circle has five points: 0°, 90°, 180°, 270°, and 360°.

0° is "Small I."

90° is "Karma I."

180° is "Nothing I"

270° is "Freedom I."

360° is "Big I."

1 ⊘ What is the meaning of "Small I"?

2 ⊘ What is the meaning of "Karma I"?

3 ⊘ What is the meaning of "Nothing I"?

4 ⊘ What is the meaning of "Big I"?

5 ⊘ "Big I" and "Small I" are at the same point. Are "Big I" and "Small I" the same or different?

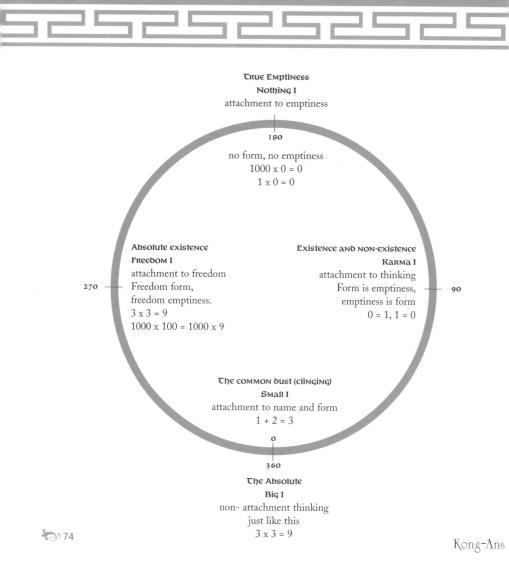

TRue Emptiness
Nothing I
attachment to emptiness

180

no form, no emptiness
$1000 \times 0 = 0$
$1 \times 0 = 0$

Absolute existence
Freedom I
attachment to freedom
Freedom form,
freedom emptiness.
$3 \times 3 = 9$
$1000 \times 100 = 1000 \times 9$

270

Existence and non-existence
Karma I
attachment to thinking
Form is emptiness,
emptiness is form
$0 = 1, 1 = 0$

90

The common dust (clinging)
Small I
attachment to name and form
$1 + 2 = 3$

0

360

The Absolute
Big I
non-attachment thinking
just like this
$3 \times 3 = 9$

| | If "Small I" disappears, what?
| | "Small I," "Karma I," "Nothing I," "Freedom I," and "Big I." Which one is true "I"?

COMMENTARY

If one mind appears then everything appears. If one mind disappears then everything disappears. All these degrees and these "I"s come from where? You already understand. But no mind, no eyes—then what? What do you see now? Is that "Big I" or "Small I"? Put it all down! Just see, just hear, and then you will get everything.

Five Schools

The Sixth Patriarch Hui Neng's two more prominent disciples, Ch'ing Yuan and Nan Yeh, gave birth to five major schools of Zen:

> *Im Je (Rinzai) School* – Whole substance, correct function is KATZ or Hit.
>
> *Un Mun School* – Body hidden in the North Star but appears in the golden wind.
>
> *Jo Dong (Soto) School* – King and subjects together, center and sides never separate.

Zen

> *Poep Ahn School* – Hear sound, attain correct way, mind
> is clear.
> *Wi Ahn School* – Teacher and student in harmony
> together. Father and son live in the same house.

1. ◔ What is the meaning of the Im Je School?
2. ◔ What is the meaning of the Un Mun School?
3. ◔ What is the meaning of the Jo Dong School?
4. ◔ What is the meaning of the Poep Ahn School?
5. ◔ What is the meaning of the Wi Ahn School?

COMMENTARY

One body, five heads. Where does it go? Go straight: Only
depend on your legs.

What Is Buddha-Nature?

The Buddha said that all things have Buddha-nature. Zen
Master Joju said that a dog has no Buddha-nature.

1. ◔ Which one is correct?
2. ◔ Which one is incorrect?
3. ◔ The ten thousand dharmas return to the One. Where
   does the One return?

The dog never says, "I am a dog." But the dog is barking.
The cat never says, "I am a cat." But the cat is meowing.
Name and form do not matter. The dog, the tree, and the
flower all understand their job, but Buddha doesn't understand Buddha's job; human beings don't understand human
being's job. Very stupid! Put it all down. What are you doing
now? Just do it. That's all.

The Human Route

Coming empty-handed, going empty-handed, that is human.
When you are born, where do you come from?
When you die, where do you go?
Life is like a floating cloud which appears.
Death is like a floating cloud which disappears.
The floating cloud itself originally does not exist.
Life and death, coming and going are also like that.
But there is one thing which always remains clear.
Is it pure and clear, not depending on life and death.
Then what is the one pure and clear thing?

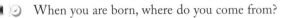

1. ⊘ When you are born, where do you come from?
2. ⊘ When you die, where do you go?
3. ⊘ What is the one pure and clear thing?

Commentary

A dog understands a dog's job, and a cat understands a cat's job. Human beings appear—what are they to do? They want fame, money, food, sex, and sleep. After that, then what? But one thing is clear. It swallows everything—the sun, the moon, the stars, the mountains, water—everything. If you do not find that, you attain "you," and freedom from life and death. Then you go drink tea.

❦

Just Seeing Is Buddha-Nature

If you want to understand the realm of Buddha, keep a mind which is clear like space. Let all thinking and external desires fall far away. Let your mind go any place, with no hindrance. Then what is keeping a mind which is clear like space? If your mind is not clear, listen to the following:

It is enlightenment-nature.
Above is the dwelling place of all Buddhas;
Below are the six realms of existence.
One by one, each thing is complete.
One by one, each thing has it.
It and dust interpenetrate.
It is already apparent in all things.
So, without cultivation, you are already complete—
Understand, understand.
Clear, clear.
(Holding the Zen stick) *Do you see?*
(Hitting with the Zen stick) *Do you hear?*
Already you see clearly. Already you hear clearly.
Then what are this stick, this sound and your mind?
Are they the same or different?
If you say "same," I will hit you thirty times.
If you say "different," I will also hit you thirty times.
Why?
KATZ!
3 x 3 = 9.

1 ☯ How do you keep a mind which is clear like space?

2 ② "Understand, understand. Clear, clear." What does this
mean?

3 ② What does "3 x 3 = 9" mean?

COMMENTARY

In the springtime, many flowers. In the summer, the trees
are green. In the fall, fruit appears. In the winter, it is very
cold. In the beginning, four legs; next, two legs; next, three
legs; next, no legs. Where do they stay? Do you understand
that? If you don't understand ask the stone girl. She will have
a good answer for you.

WHERE ARE YOU GOING?

Ancient Buddhas went like this.
Present Buddhas go like this.
You go like this.
I also go like this.
What is the thing that is not broken?
Who is eternally indestructible?
Do you understand?

> *In the three worlds,*
> *all Buddhas of the past, present, and future*
> *simultaneously become the Path.*
> *On the ten levels,*
> *all beings on the same day enter Nirvana.*

If you don't understand this, check the following:

> *The statue has eyes and tears silently drip down.*
> *The boy sniffles wordlessly in the dark.*

1. ⟳ Who is eternally indestructible?
2. ⟳ What do the following sentences mean?
   a. In the three worlds, all Buddhas of past, present, and future simultaneously become the Path.
   b. The statue has eyes and tears silently drip down.
   c. The boy sniffles wordlessly in the dark.

COMMENTARY

Where does mind come from? Where does it go? Originally there is no name and no form. Open your mouth, everything appears. Close your mouth, everything disappears. If you have no mouth, then what? If you don't understand, go ask the gold Buddha-statue. He will teach you.

43

ZEN MASTER TO SOL'S THREE GATES

Zen Master To Sol had three gates:

1. Cutting ignorance grass and sitting Zen is wishing to see nature. Then where is your nature now?
2. You already understand nature and pass beyond life and death. When you die, how will you be reborn?
3. You already have freedom over life and death and also understand where you return to. When the four elements disperse, where do you go?

COMMENTARY

Coming empty-handed, going empty-handed—that is human. What are empty hands? Where do these empty hands come from? Who made this? When thinking appears, everything appears. If you have no thinking, where will you stay? Put it all down. What are you doing now? If you are thirsty, go drink cold water.

Freedom From Life and Death

> *Under the sea, a running cow eats the moon.*
> *In front of the rock, the stone tiger sleeps, holding a*
>   *baby in his arms.*
> *The steel snake drills into the eye of a diamond.*
> *Mount Kun-Lun rides on the back of an elephant*
>   *pulled by a little bird.*

Which of these sentences is freedom from life and death?

Commentary

If you want something then you lose everything. If you don't want anything then you already have everything. But you must hear the stone lion roaring. Then the whole world is in your hand. You can be free and can do anything.

Quiet Night, the Geese Cry

> *Sitting silently in a mountain temple in the quiet night,*
> *Extreme quiet and stillness are original naturalness.*
> *Why does the Western wind shake the forest?*
> *A single cry of the cold-weather geese fills the sky.*

1 ⊘ "Extreme quiet and stillness are original naturalness." What does this mean?

2 ⊘ "Why does the Western wind shake the forest?" What does this mean?

3 ⊘ "A single cry of the cold-weather geese fills the sky." What does this mean?

COMMENTARY

Bodhidharma came from the West. The Eastern world had many problems, so he sat in Sorim for nine years. That was a big mistake. But this mistake fixed all human beings' mistake. For cold sickness, use cold medicine; hot sickness, use hot medicine. So Bodhidharma's mistake fixed all human beings' mistake. What kind of mistake did Bodhidharma make? Three years after he died, he was alive again, and returned to the West. Where is Bodhidharma now? In front of you the pine tree is green.

Zen Master Ko Bong's Three Gates

1. ⊘ The sun in the sky shines everywhere. Why does a cloud obscure it?
2. ⊘ Everyone has a shadow following them, How can you not step on your shadow?
3. ⊘ The whole universe is on fire. Through what kind of samhadi can you escape being burned?

Commentary

The sun, the moon, the stars, the mountains and waters—everything is complete. One mind appears, big mistake. One mind disappears, then seeing and hearing become the truth. Don't make anything. Just see, just hear, just do it.

Just Like This Is Buddha

The Compass of Zen says:

> The spirit remains clear and light.
> The six roots (senses) and the six dusts (perceptions)
>   are taken off and thrown away.
> The original body remains clear constantly.

Speech and words cannot hinder it.
True nature has no taint and is already a perfect sphere
Only without thinking, just like this is Buddha.

1 "The original body remains clear constantly." What does this mean?

2 "True nature has no taint." What does this mean?

3 "Only without thinking, just like this is Buddha." What does this mean?

COMMENTARY

Everything is already complete, but human beings have one mouth and two eyes. That is a mistake. If you have no sixth consciousness, then are the tree and the rocks the same or different? Don't check, just do it. Then you are better than Buddha.

48

WHERE ARE the BUDDHA AND the EMINENT TEACHERS?

The four elements (earth, water, fire, and air) disperse as in a dream.

The six dusts (perceptions), roots (senses), and consciousnesses are originally empty.

> To understand that, the Buddha and the Eminent
> Teachers return to the place of light:
> The sun is setting over the western mountains.
> The moon is rising in the east.

1 🕉 The six dusts, roots, and consciousness all disappear.
   Then what?

2 🕉 Where are the Buddha and the Eminent Teachers?

3 🕉 Before the sun sets, before the moon rises—what?

COMMENTARY

One man has no use for the Buddha. He sees clearly and
hears clears. He never checks, never holds, and is not attached
to anything. You, too, just eat, just work, just sleep, just do it.
Then all Buddhas become your attendants. How wonderful!

49

Why Are You Saying These Bad Things About Me?

Ko Bong Sunim had been drinking too much liquor. He went
to his room and lay down and began saying bad things about his
teacher, Zen Master Man Gong. "Man Gong doesn't understand anything. …He's not correct. …His speech is bullshit."

Just then, Man Gong walked past Ko Bong's room and

heard him. He opened the door and shouted, "Ko Bong, why are you saying these bad things about me?"

Surprised, Ko Bong sat up and said, "Zen Master, I am not saying any bad things about you. I am only saying these things about Man Gong."

The Zen Master asked, "Man Gong and me, are they the same or different?"

Ko Bong shouted, "KATZ!"

Man Gong smiled. "You've had too much to drink. Now go to sleep."

1 ⊘ "Man Gong and me, are they the same or different?" What does this mean?

2 ⊘ Ko Bong shouted, "KATZ!" How many pounds does it weigh?

COMMENTARY

Ko Bong thinks about this world as if it were a small coin. He sees the road as if it were a thread. All Buddhas and Bodhisattvas are his attendants. His teacher, Man Gong, is like a baby. So, Ko Bong is a great, free person. But he doesn't understand one thing: his condition. He only understands his situation. So who can take care of him? A stone girl appears. She shouts at him, "You must sleep!" Ko Bong only says, "Yes, Ma'am," and goes to sleep.

Ko Bong's Enlightenment

One summer, before he became a great Zen Master, Ko Bong Sunim sat summer Kyol Che at Tong Do Sah Temple. It was very hot that summer, so many retreatants could not stay in the meditation hall. Some sat on the veranda, some sat under the trees, while others sat by a nearby stream. Ko Bong sat on some rocks, under a big tree, courageously keeping don't-know mind one hundred percent. Above him, a cicada was singing in the tree. Ko Bong heard that and instantly his mind opened—he got enlightenment. He hit the rocks with a fan and the fan broke. "That's it!" he shouted, laughing, "Ha, ha, ha, ha, ha, ha!"

1 Ko Bong heard the cicada's song and got enlightenment. What did he attain?

2 He hit the rocks with a fan and broke the fan, then

shouted, "That's it!" What does this mean?

3 ⊙ Loud laughter. "Ha, ha, ha, ha, ha, ha!" What does this mean?

COMMENTARY

One day, sometime before this summer Kyol Che, Ko Bong visited Tong Do Sah Temple. He stood at the gate and shouted, "Somebody come here and cut my hair, please. I want to become a monk." Many monks were angered by his arrogant behavior. They grabbed some sticks and went out to beat him. Ko Bong only said, "You can hit my body but you cannot hit my mind. If you can hit my mind, I will become your disciple." But none of the monks could hit his mind.

Another time, outside Nam Ja Sah Temple, he shouted the same kinds of things, and again all of the monks were very angry and wanted to beat him. Ko Bong again asked if anyone could hit his mind. At that time, Zen Master Hae Bong heard this and came to see Ko Bong. He asked, "How many pounds does your mind weigh?" Ko Bong could not answer, so he cut off all his hair and became a monk.

51

夜 夜 抱 佛 眠

My Cow Is Not This Small, My Cow Is Bigger

One summer, Ko Bong Sunim sat Kyol Che at Won Sah Temple, where the famous Zen Master Hae Wol was teaching. There were thirty monks sitting mornings and evenings, and working in the garden during the day. The work was hard and they were all very tired by evening. Also, they had no money and very little food, and the food that they had was awful. There were many complaints among the monks.

One morning, Zen Master Hae Wol left his students for a few days to visit the head temple. After he left, Ko Bong talked his fellow monks into selling the temple's cow. (They needed this cow for work in the garden, so without it, they would not be able to work.) After selling the cow, Ko Bong suggested they buy good food and drink for everyone. That night, instead of sitting, they had a big party. They ate, drank, shouted, danced, and sang songs. They were very happy. They went to sleep quite late and did not get up for morning chanting.

As he returned to the temple early the next morning, with the sun already rising, the Zen Master could not hear any chanting. He noticed that the cow was missing. Upon opening the temple door, he was hit with the bad smell from all he food and drink. His students lay all about, snoring loudly.

Perceiving what they had done, he became very angry and shouted, "Wake up! Wake up!!" Everyone jumped up, very afraid, but could say nothing. Walking toward the Buddha statue, he looked from student to student. His eyes were big, like a lion's. "Who stole my cow?" he shouted. Everyone jumped nervously, and became even more afraid. But they said nothing. They all just looked at Ko Bong Sunim. For his part, Ko Bong just sat there. He was not afraid. Again the Zen Master shouted, "Who stole my cow?"

Suddenly, Ko Bong stood up and removed all his clothes. Getting down on his hands and knees he crawled in front of Hae Wol, saying, "Moo! Moooo!"

Zen Master Hae Wol only smiled, and hit Ko Bong on his bare ass, saying, "My cow is not this small." Hitting him again, he added, "My cow is bigger."

Then Ko Bong got up and returned to his room. The cow was never mentioned again.

1 ⊘ Ko Bong said, "Moo!" What did he mean?

2 ⊘ Ko Bong's body and the cow's body — are they the same or different?

3 Why did the Zen Master never mention the cow again?

COMMENTARY

If you are not attached to anything, then you are free. If you hold something you are hindered. When you see, when you hear, and when you smell, you are never separate from the universe. But when thinking appears, then everything falls away and becomes separated. So when you are hungry, eat; when you are tired, sleep. Then you are already better than Buddhas and Bodhisattvas.

52 Big Bell Ceremony

One day at Su Dok Sah Temple they were having a grand ceremony to dedicate the big new temple bell. Zen Master Hae Am stepped up to give the Dharma speech, saying, "We now have a big bell. Is this bell outside or inside your mind? When you hear the bell, stand up. When you hear the drum, fall down. What does this mean?"

No one answered. Then he said, "I will give you the answer." He clenched his hand in a fist and held it up. "If this is correct…

pening his hand, "then this is not correct."

- ◎ Is this bell outside or inside your mind?
- ◎ "When you hear the bell, stand up. When you hear the drum, fall down." What does this mean?
- ◎ Zen Master Hae Am clenched his hand in a fist and held it up. "If this is correct…" opening his hand, "then this is not correct." What does this mean?

OMMENTARY

Zen Master Hae Am was very clever and very stupid. He pened his mouth, and it was already a mistake. The stone rl hit him thirty times. Do you know the true meaning of is? When Hae Am gave his Dharma speech all the Buddhas d Bodhisattvas faced west and said, "Great Zen Master is in ont of you at this moment."

traight Line in the Circle

The great layman Hwa Ryon Gosa received *inga* from en Master Ko Bong.* One day, a student asked him,

ga signifies a Zen master's "seal" or approval of a student to teach ng-an practice.

"What is Dharma?"

He answered by making a circle in the air.

The student said, "I still don't understand."

Hwa Ryon Gosa replied, "In the circle there is one place where there is a straight line, not curved. Where is that place?" The student still could not understand, so Hwa Ryon Gosa told him, "You must sit more."

1 ⊘ Hwa Ryon Gosa made a circle in the air. What does this mean?

2 ⊘ In the circle, where is the straight line?

COMMENTARY

The earth goes around the sun; the moon goes around the earth. They never stop, and they never go straight. But these things originally have no name and no form, and they are unmoving. When mind appears, everything appears; when mind disappears, everything disappears. When mind does not appear or disappear, then what? Then everything is straight.

Before the Donkey Has Left, the Horse Has Already Arrived

A long time ago, Mun Ik asked Manjushri Bodhisattva, "How many students do you have?"

"In front three, in back three, three," Manjushri replied.

Zen Master Hae Am's commentary was:

> Before the donkey has left,
> the horse already arrived.

1. ☺ What is the meaning of "In front three, in back three, three"?

2. ☺ "Before the donkey has left, the horse has already arrived." What does this mean?

3. ☺ Hae Am's commentary is like scratching his right foot when his left foot itches. How can you make it correct?

COMMENTARY

In the sky, there are many stars and moons and suns. On the ground there are many mountains, rivers, oceans, and houses. How many are there? If you understand, you become Buddha. Zen Master Hae Am had a big mouth and said, "Before the donkey has left, the horse has already

arrived." But Hae Am had no mouth, so how could he say that? Silence is better than holiness.

55 SWORD MOUNTAIN

人

劍

一

Young Master So Sahn visited old Zen Master Tu Ja, who asked him, "Where are you coming from?"

So Sahn answered, "From Sword Mountain."

"Then did you bring your sword?"

"Yes, I did."

"Then show it to this old monk." So Sahn pointed one finger to the ground in front of Tu Ja, who abruptly stood up and left the room.

Later that afternoon, Tu Ja asked his attendant to invite So Sahn to have a cup of tea with him. The attendant told him that after the morning's event, So Sahn had left immediately.

Tu Ja then sang a gatha:

"For thirty years I have ridden horseback,

And today I was kicked from the horse by a small donkey."

1 ☺ When the monk asked, "Did you bring your sword?" the young monk pointed to the ground. If you were the old monk, what could you do?

2 ⊙ So Sahn pointed to the ground. What does this mean?

3 ⊙ "Today I was kicked from the horse by a small donkey." What does this mean?

COMMENTARY

Beware of this donkey. If you open your mouth, then the donkey has already kicked you. If you close your mouth, then he has also kicked you. What can you do?

The donkey already kicked Master So Sahn. Tu Ja was already on horseback. But this donkey kicked both monks out of this world. How can they find their bodies? All that appears is sound, "Aigo, aigo, aigo!"

56

Give Me a Don't-Know Sentence

Once, when Zen Master Man Gong was staying at Jeong Hae Sah Temple, a student came to his room, bowed, and said, "Zen Master, since I came to this temple, I have understood many things. So today, I ask you to give me a don't-know sentence."

Without a moment's hesitation, Man Gong thrust his fist to within a half inch of the student's face. The student gasped

nd instantly attained enlightenment. He bowed deeply and
aid, "Thank you for your teaching."

1. ⊙ What did the student attain?
2. ⊙ Give me a don't-know sentence.
3. ⊙ Man Gong punched his fist to within a half inch of the
student's face. What does this mean?

Commentary

Socrates used to walk through the streets and markets of
Athens, telling people as he passed, "You must understand
your true self." One of his students asked him, "Teacher, do
you understand your true self?" "I don't know," he replied, "but
I understand this don't-know." Man Gong's action and
Socrates' action, are they the same or different? If you attain
that, then you attain your true self. If you don't understand, go
to the kitchen and drink cold water.

Zen Teachings and Sutra Teachings

Someone asked Zen Master Pa Ling, "Are Zen teachings
and Sutra teachings the same or different?"

Pa Ling replied, "When a chicken is cold, it goes into a tree. When a duck is cold, it goes under water."

Zen Master Hae Am's commentary on this is, "Even though water is flowing, sound cannot be seen."

1 🕗 Are Zen teachings and Sutra teachings the same or different?

2 🕗 "When a chicken is cold, it goes into a tree. When a duck is cold, it goes under water." What does this mean?

3 🕗 "Even though water is flowing, sound cannot be seen." What does this mean?

COMMENTARY

The ten thousand dharmas return to the One. Where does the One return to? If you attain that point, then is that Sutra or Zen teaching? If you say "Zen," you have already received thirty blows. If you say "Sutra," then you have also received thirty blows. What can you do? Tell me, tell me! If you don't understand, go drink tea.

True Nature Does Not Exist

Manjushri Bodhisattva sent a poem to Precepts Master Chan Jang:

> *"When you understand all Dharmas,*
> *True nature does not exist.*
> *Understand that Dharma nature*
> *Is just like this.*
> *Then you see Nosahna* Buddha."*

In this poem there is one word which is beyond life and death, beyond mind and Buddha, so it is freedom from life and death.

1. ☺ "True Nature does not exist." What does this mean?
2. ☺ "Dharma nature is just like this." What does this mean?
3. ☺ Which word is freedom from life and death?

COMMENTARY

When the wind blows from the east, the clouds move west. When the wind blows from the west, the clouds move east. No wind, no clouds, no moon, no sun. Then what? See this, become Buddha.

* Highest Buddha.

59

花
笑
佛
不
安

Speech, Silence, Moving, Quiet

One day Zen Master Man Gong and Zen Master Yong Song were standing together at Son Ha Won Temple in Seoul

Yong Song asked Man Gong, "Give me a sentence without speech, silence, moving, or quiet."

Man Gong acted as if he hadn't heard.

"Isn't that silence?" Yong Song asked.

"No."

The other people there could not understand who was correct. Later, Zen Master Jun Kang heard of this exchange and said, "It is as though both masters fell into muddy water while fighting with each other."

Zen Master Hae Am commented, "If someone asked me for one sentence without speech, silence, moving, or quiet, I would say: 'A broken bowl cannot be put back into its original condition.'"

1 ☺ What is silence?

2 ☺ Someone asks you, "Give me one sentence without speech, silence, moving, or quiet." What can you do?

3 ☺ Zen Master Man Gong said, "No." What does this mean?

4 ☺ Zen Master Jun Kang said, "It is as though both masters fell into muddy water while fighting with each

other." What does this mean?

Zen Master Hae Am said, "If someone asked me for one sentence without speech, silence, moving, or quiet, I would say: 'A broken bowl cannot be put back into its original condition.'" What does this mean?

COMMENTARY

All the Zen Masters are wrestling together in the mud. Where are their eyes, noses, mouths, hands, and legs? Which one is Man Gong? Which one is Yong Song? Which is Jun Kang? Hae Am? They cannot be distinguished. Who made a mistake?

The sky never says, "I am the sky." The tree never says, "I am a tree." The dog only barks, "Woof, woof." If you open your mouth, you get thirty blows; if you close your mouth, then you also get thirty blows. What can you do? Put it all down. If you are thirsty, go drink some cold water.

The True Meaning of the Cypress Tree in the Garden

A long time ago in China, someone asked Zen Master Joju, "Why did Bodhidharma come to China?" "The

cypress tree in the garden," he replied. Years later, Zen Master Song Sang commented:

> "Fish moving, water becomes cloudy.
> Bird flies, a feather falls."

Many Zen Masters have offered commentaries on Song Sang's verse. Zen Master Hae Am commented:

> "Self-nature is already clear.
> Mind-moving is already a big mistake."

1. *Joju said, "The cypress tree in the garden." What does this mean?*

2. *Song Sang said, "Fish moving, water becomes cloudy. Bird flies, a feather falls." Where is his mistake? Where is there not a mistake?*

3. *"Self-nature is already clear. Mind moving is already a big mistake." That is only an explanation. What is the true meaning?*

COMMENTARY

Zen Masters Hae Am and Song Sang are wrestling with each other. They hit and kick each other. Blood is flowing; their faces are broken and bruised. But they still don't understand why they are wrestling. The cypress tree is clearly in ront of you in the garden.

So why are they wrestling together? They have no eyes and no consciousness. In the clear mirror, red comes—red is reflected; white comes—white. Don't make anything. Just see it, just do it. This is better than opening your mouth. Watch your step!

Ten Sicknesses

When Zen Master Yong Song was staying at Man Wol Sah Temple, he sent a letter to several other temples in Korea which said, "In the 'Mu' kong-an, there are ten sicknesses. Please send me one sentence without the ten sicknesses."

Zen Master Man Gong answered, "A monk asked Zen Master Joju, 'Does a dog have Buddha-nature?' Joju said, 'Mu.'" Yong Song replied to Man Gong, "An iron hammer without a hole."

Zen Master Hae Am answered, "Already fell down. What can you do?"

Zen Master Hae Wol answered, "KATZ! Is that correct or not?"

Zen Master Song Wol wrote from Kun Jung Mountain, "On top of Man Wol Mountain [where Yong Song was] is a

cloud. Under Kun Jung Mountain is a thief."

1. ⦿ Joju said, "Mu." What does this mean?
2. ⦿ Where are the "mu" kong-an's ten sicknesses?
3. ⦿ Give me one sentence without the ten sicknesses.

Commentary

On the mountain there are many trees, in the ocean, there are many fish. They all have different names and forms, but everything returns to one point. What is that? If you find this one point then this kong-an is no problem. In the clear mirror, red comes—red is reflected; white comes—white. If you are not holding anything and not checking anything, then your mind is clear like space. If you're thinking and checking, then this kong-an is a thousand miles away. Be careful!

The Burning Fire

You are the burning fire,
I the reflected glow.
How could I without you
and you without me grow?

62

1 ◎ Who are you?
2 ◎ What does "I the reflected glow" mean?
3 ◎ "You without me grow." What does this mean?
4 ◎ You and me, are they the same or different?

COMMENTARY

Mind appears, you and I are separate. Mind disappears, you and I are never separate.

63

All As Nothingness

Who sees the All as nothingness,
as nothing all that is,
sees everything through God's own eye.
Enlightenment is this.

1 ◎ You are nothingness. So how do you see nothingness?
2 ◎ What is the meaning of "God's own eye"?
3 ◎ What does enlightenment mean?

COMMENTARY

Open your mouth and everything appears. Close your mouth, nothing appears. So stillness is better than bliss. But be careful! Don't be attached to emptiness and stillness.

Pure Emptiness

The God who is pure emptiness
is created as form,
becoming substance, light and darkness,
the stillness and the storm.

◎ What is the meaning of "pure emptiness"?

◎ What is the meaning of "becoming substance"?

Commentary

KATZ! Is that God or is that substance? If you say substance, you go to hell; if you say God you are already dead.

64

The Deepest Well

You are the deepest well
from which all rises, grows.
You are the boundless ocean
back into which all flows.

◎ What does "the deepest well" mean?

◎ What does "boundless ocean" mean?

65

COMMENTARY

How wide is your mind? How deep? If you understand this, you meet God face-to-face.

GOD INSIDE GOD

> *I was God inside God*
> *before this timebound ME,*
> *and shall be God again*
> *When from my ME set free.*

1 ☺ "I was God inside God." What does this mean?

2 ☺ When will your ME be set free?

COMMENTARY

God made everything, so everything has God-nature. If mind appears, you lose God-nature. But if you take away mind, you are always sitting with God.

Empty Becoming

> *The emptier I do become,*
> *the more delivered from the Me,*
> *the better shall I understand*
> *what is God's liberty.*

- ☉ If you are empty, how do you "become"?
- ☉ How do you understand "God's liberty"?

Commentary

One mind never appeared. God and you are never separate.
When your mind appears, you must believe in God one hundred percent.

No True One Is Elated

> *By honors and by titles*
> *no true one is elated.*
> *To realize that which we are,*
> *for this we were created.*

- ☉ "No true one is elated." What does this mean?
- ☉ Why were we created?

The sun, the moon, the stars—where do they come from?
If you attain this point, you can see God's face.

Jesus Christ

*However well of Jesus Christ
you talk and sermons preach,
unless he lives within yourself,
he is beyond your reach.*

⊘ Who is Jesus Christ?

⊘ How does he live within you?

⊘ How do you reach him?

Commentary

The Cross sets you free. If you attain the Cross, you sit
together with God.

Without a Single Law

> *The precepts are only for the wicked.*
> *Without a single law,*
> *the just will love all living things,*
> *holding God's life in awe.*

1 ◎ "The just will love all living things." What does this mean?
2 ◎ How do you hold God's life in awe?

Commentary

The sky is blue, the water is flowing. If you attain the true meaning of this, God smiles on you.

The Nightingale and the Cuckoo

> *The Nightingale does not resent*
> *the Cuckoo's simple song.*
> *But you, if I don't sing like you,*
> *tell me that I am wrong.*

1 ◎ What is the meaning of "The Cuckoo's simple song"?
2 ◎ Why doesn't the Nightingale resent it?

COMMENTARY

Dog barking, "Woof, woof!" Chicken crowing, "Cock-a-doodle-doo!"

Inside, Outside

If you go out, God will come in.
So die—in God withdraw.
Not-being, you will be in God,
not-doing, you will live in God's law.

1. ◎ Who makes inside and outside?
2. ◎ Is God inside or outside your mind?
3. ◎ What is "not-being"?
4. ◎ What is "not-doing"?

COMMENTARY

Coming or going, God is never separate from you. If you laugh, God is happy; if you cry, God is sad.

72 世風起浪

73

Christ's Birth and Death

> *Christ was born human for me*
> *and for me he died.*
> *If I don't get transformed in God*
> *His birth is mocked, His death denied.*

1. Does Christ have life and death?
2. Before Christ was born, who took care of you?

Commentary

The blue sky is Christ's face. The blue mountain is His body.

74

The Rose Blooms

> *The rose blooms because she blooms,*
> *she never asks WHY?*
> *Nor does she preen herself*
> *to catch my wandering eye.*

1. Why does the rose bloom?
2. How does the rose catch your wandering eye?

COMMENTARY

The child wants to catch the butterfly. The fisherman sinks his bait into the water.

75

The Nature of All Things

If to the nature of all things
you wish to penetrate,
You will know all, if you can find
the door to just one thing.

1 How do you penetrate all things?

2 Where is the door to just one thing?

COMMENTARY

Your face cannot see your face. Nature cannot see nature. If you want to see your face, it's already a big mistake; nature understanding nature is also a big mistake. How do you see your face? How do you understand nature? Be careful, be careful! Dog laughing outside, "Woof, woof!"

Achievements Perish

> *All you achieved and stored in barns*
> *must perish in the end.*
> *Therefore, became that which you are*
> *and which the world transcends.*

1. If everything perishes in the end, where do you stay?
2. What does "the world transcends" mean?

Commentary

What you see now—is that God? What you hear now—is that God? If you attain this point, you will become free.

No Fear of Death

> *The wise have no fear of death,*
> *too often they have died*
> *to Ego and its vanities,*
> *to all that keeps them tied.*

1. When you die, where do you go?
2. If you are not tied to anything, then what?

Commentary

You must pay for the rental car when you return it.

78 Always in Paradise

> *No thought for the hereafter*
> *is cherished by the wise.*
> *For on this earth they truly live*
> *always in paradise.*

1. How do you not think about the hereafter?
2. What is the meaning of "always in paradise"?

Commentary

When desire appears, hell and paradise appear. When desire disappears, hell and paradise disappear.

79 The Deepest Prayer

> *The deepest prayer on this earth*
> *that anyone could say*
> *is that which makes me wholly One*
> *with that to which I pray.*

1 🌀 When praying, how do you become one with prayer?

2 🌀 What is the deepest prayer?

Commentary

The mother rubs her child's stomach. The priest prays in church.

At the Soul's Center

*Unless you find the paradise
at your soul's very center,
you haven't got the smallest chance
that you can once there enter.*

1 🌀 Where is the soul's center?

2 🌀 How do you enter paradise?

Commentary

Originally, there is no name and no form, so where is south, east, west, and north? If you attain this point, you attain the standing place.

Redemption

Christians are foolish thinking
they can attain redemption
while with their bodies and their souls
remain attached to worldly goals.

1 ⊙ How can you attain redemption?

2 ⊙ How do you take away attachments to worldly goals?

Commentary

Don't make anything, don't want anything. Then the universe will give you everything.

Old Clothes

One day Zen Master Hyang Gok put on very old, tattered clothes and visited several temples. At one temple, Zen Master Ko Bong saw him and asked, "How can you fix those old clothes?"

1 ⊙ If you were Hyang Gok, how would you answer?

2 ⊙ How much do Hyang Gok's clothes weigh?

In winter, you must use heavy winter clothes. In summer, use light summer clothes.

The Meaning of Am Du's Whispering

83

When Zen Master Hyang Gok visited Zen Master Jun Kang at Dae Gak Sah Temple, he asked Jun Kang, "What is the meaning of Am Du's whispering in the master's ear?"

"Even the Buddha and the Bodhisattvas do not understand," Jun Kang replied. "How can I understand?"

Hyang Gok cried out and left.

Then Jun Kang called out to him, "If you do not believe me, I will give you another answer."

Hyang Gok said, "I don't give acupuncture to a dead cow," and continued on his way.

Sometime later, Hyang Gok's student, Jin Jae Sunim, heard about this exchange and commented, "Ma Jo killed everybody Lin Chi is not yet stupid."

1 ⊘   Hyang Gok cried out and left. What does this mean?

- "I don't give acupuncture to a dead cow." What does this mean?
- Jin Jae answered, "Ma Jo killed everybody. Lin Chi is not yet stupid." Is this correct or not?

COMMENTARY

Three people fight in a muddy place, hit each other, and become dirty.

84

Whose Song Do You Sing?

One day, Jin Jae Sunim asked his teacher, Zen Master Hyang Gok, "Whose song do you sing? Whose lineage do you follow?"

Hyang Gok replied, "I received one word from Zen Master Un Mun and I have never exhausted it."

- Whose song do you sing?
- Whose lineage do you follow?
- Is Hyang Gok's answer correct or not?

COMMENTARY

The sky is clear: Why is there lightning?

Zen

Money to Spend

Jin Jae Sunim persisted, "Only that? Not more?"

Zen Master Hyang Gok answered, "I have a lot of money in my pocket. In heaven and on earth, coming or going, I am free to spend it."

1. ◎ If you were Hyang Gok, how would you answer?
2. ◎ Is Hyang Gok's answer correct or not?
3. ◎ Hyang Gok said, "I have a lot of money in my pocket." What kind of money did Hyang Gok have?

COMMENTARY

Hyang Gok has a hole in his pocket, so he loses all his money.

What Is Your True Speech?

Jin Jae Sunim asked Zen Master Hyang Gok, "What is your true speech?"

Zen Master Hyang Gok said, "The cry of a mud cow appeared. Heaven and earth are surprised. The Buddha and eminent teachers are all dead."

1. ◎ What is your true speech?

2 🕑 Is Zen Master Hyang Gok's speech true?

3 🕑 Did you hear the cry of the mud cow?

COMMENTARY

In last night's dream, a golden cow was riding in a chariot. The golden cow said, "Woof, woof!"

87

WHEN ONE IS PICKED UP, SEVEN ARE GOTTEN

Jin Jae Sunim asked Zen Master Hyang Gok, "What is your special technique?"

Hyang Gok answered, "When one is picked up, seven are gotten."

1 🕑 What is your special technique?

2 🕑 What is the meaning of "When one is picked up, seven are gotten"?

3 🕑 One and seven come from where?

COMMENTARY

Facing the ground, pick up the moon.

First Word

Jin Jae Sunim asked Zen Master Hyang Gok, "What is the first word?"

Hyang Gok answered, "Shakyamuni Buddha and Maitreya Bodhisattva fell into quicksand."

88

1.  What is the first word?
2.  What is the meaning of "Shakyamuni Buddha and Maitreya Bodhisattva fell into quicksand"?
3.  Is Hyang Gok's answer correct or not?

Commentary

Opening your mouth is a mistake as big as Sumi Mountain. Close your mouth, you're already in hell.

Last Word

Jin Jae Sunim asked Zen Master Hyang Gok, "What is the last word?"

89

Zen Master Hyang Gok said, "In the lightning, tripped and fell down."

1.  What is the last word?

2 ☯ "In the lightning, tripped and fell down." What does
this mean?

COMMENTARY

Head is facing the sky, legs are pointing toward the ground

Tathagata Zen

Jin Jae Sunim asked Zen Master Hyang Gok, "What is
Tathagata Zan?"

Hyang Gok answered, "Keen-eyed students fall into the well."

1 ☯ What is Tathagata Zen?

2 ☯ Is Hyang Gok's answer correct or not?

3 ☯ If you are a keen-eyed student, how do you fall into
the well?

COMMENTARY

Two legs, two hands, one head.

Going-Up Sentence

Jin Jae Sunim asked Zen Master Hyang Gok, "What is a 'going-up' sentence?"

Hyang Gok answered, "The Buddha and all eminent teachers fell into the fire."

⊘ What is a "going-up" sentence?

⊘ Is Hyang Gok's answer correct or not?

COMMENTARY

Cloud floating in the sky, water flowing underground.

Coming-Down Sentence

Jin Jae Sunim asked Zen Master Hyang Gok, "What is a 'coming-down' sentence?"

Hyang Gok answered, "A stone man rides an iron cow past a jeweled world."

1 ⊘ What is a "coming-down" sentence?

2 ⊘ What does Hyang Gok's answer mean?

3 ⊘ Is Hyang Gok's answer correct? If not, how do you make it correct?

COMMENTARY

In last night's dream, the stone girl got lots of money and built a temple.

Changing-Body Sentence

Jin Jae Sunim asked Zen Master Hyang Gok, "What is a 'changing-body' sentence?"

Hyang Gok answered, "Three heads and six arms, swallowing and spitting freely."

1. What is a "changing-body" sentence?
2. "Three heads and six arms, swallowing and spitting freely." What does this mean?
3. Is Hyang Gok's answer correct?

COMMENTARY

In the sky, clouds change into rain that falls down to the ground.

93

94

How Do You Catch the Sound of a Cicada?

One day, Zen Master Man Gong and some of his students were eating watermelon at Po Dok Sah Temple. Man Gong said, "If you can bring me the sound of a cicada, this watermelon is free. If you cannot, you must pay for it."

One monk made a sound with his mouth. One monk made a circle on the ground and, sitting in the center, said, "In form no Buddha, in Buddha no form." Another monk pretended to move like a cicada. The monks gave many different answers, but Man Gong only said, "No! No! NO!!!"

Finally, Bo Wol Sunim answered correctly. Man Gong smiled happily and said, "You understand my mind."

1 ☺ If you were there, what could you do?

2 ☺ What was Bo Wol Sunim's answer?

COMMENTARY

Hear sound, become deaf. Open your mouth, become mute. When seeing, become blind.

Tail of a Golden Fish

While staying at Dae Sung Sah Temple, Zen Master Kum Bong sent a letter to Zen Master Man Gong which said, "I want to fish for a golden fish's tail. Do you approve?"

Man Gong sent a letter back saying, "It's okay if you catch the tail of a golden fish, but can you eat it?"

⊘ What is the meaning of catching a golden fish's tail?

⊘ If Man Gong asked you, "Can you eat it," what could you do?

COMMENTARY

Beware, beware! A golden fish already ate up two masters.

Right in Front of You

One day a student asked Zen Master Man Gong, "Where is the Buddha's Dharma?"

"Right in front of you."

The student replied, "You say, 'In front of you,' but I cannot see it."

"You have 'I,' so you cannot see."

"Do you see?" the student asked.

Man Gong answered, "If you make 'I,' you cannot see. But if you make 'you,' it is even more difficult to see."

"If I have no 'I,' no 'you,' then who is speaking?

The student was instantly enlightened.

1 ⊘ What does "right in front of you" mean?

2 ⊘ No "I," no "you." How do you see?

3 ⊘ What did the student attain?

COMMENTARY

Stupid, stupid, stupid like a rockhead! You must see clearly hear clearly.

97

Tea Cup

One day Man Gong Sunim was drinking tea with Zen Master Su Wol. In the middle of their conversation, Su Wol picked up a tea cup and said, "Don't say this is a tea cup. Don't say this is not a tea cup. What can you say?" Man Gong answered correctly, so Su Wol was very happy.

1 ⊘ If you were there, what could you answer?

Kong-An

A monk likes noodles and cake. Laypeople like beautiful clothes and shoes.

Crying in Front of the Gate

Zen Master Hae Bong visited Zen Master Man Gong and, standing in front of the gate, cried three times, "Aigo! Aigo! Aigo!" Man Gong got up from his cushion, lay down on his bed, and correctly answered him. The Hae Bong clapped his hands and laughed, "Ha! Ha! Ha!" Upon hearing this, Man Gong instantly got out of bed and answered him again.

○ What was Man Gong's first answer?

○ What was Man Gong's second answer?

COMMENTARY

Man Gong and Hae Bong fall into the ocean upside down.

Throwing Rocks

One day, Zen Master Man Gong San visited Zen Master Hahn Am at Oh Dae Mountain's Stillness Palace Temple. When it was time for Man Gong to leave, they crossed a bridge together. Man Gong picked up a rock and threw it in front of Hahn Am, whereupon Hahn Am picked up a rock and threw it into the water.

"On this trip, much was lost," Man Gong said to himself.

◎ If you had been there, what could you have done?

◎ Zen Master Hahn Am threw a rock into the water. What does this mean?

◎ Man Gong said, "On this trip, much was lost." What does this mean?

Commentary

Don't make anything. Don't hold anything. Then, when you see, when you hear—that is better than Buddha.

100

KO BONG'S MASTER

Even before he became a great Zen teacher, the Chinese Master Ko Bong understood many kong-ans. One day, Zen Master Ang Sahn asked him this question: "In your everyday life while you are walking, sitting, and talking, is your master clear?"

"Yes, my master is very clear."

"Then I ask you, when you are completely asleep, so deeply that you're not even dreaming, and have no mind, when you cannot see or hear; at that time, where is your master then?"

Ko Bong was completely stuck, and could not answer. He decided only to practice with this question, resolving never to quit, even if it drove him completely crazy. Six years passed. Then one night, as they were doing a walking pilgrimage to the North of China, Ko Bong and a friend stopped at an inn. His friend went straight to sleep, but Ko Bong stayed up to meditate through the night. Suddenly, as his friend moved in his sleep, his wooden pillow dropped to the floor. Ko Bong heard that noise, and got enlightenment. At last, he understood not only the kong-an his teacher had given him, but all the kong-ans handed down by Buddha and the eminent teachers.

1 ⊙ When you are awake and when you are dreaming—

is your master the same or different?

2 What is your master when you are awake?

3 What is your master when you are dreaming?

4 When you are in a deep sleep, where there is no dream and no mind, where is your master?

COMMENTARY

Eyes have eyes job, ears have ears job, mouth has mouth job, mind has mind job. If you have no eyes, no ears, no mouth, and no mind, then what kind of job do you have? If you still cannot find your job, then go drink tea.

AN OLD LOAN

Zen Master Man Gong sent a letter to Zen Master Hahn Am. "We have not seen each other in ten years," he wrote. "The clouds, the full moon, the mountain, and the water everywhere are the same, but I think about you staying in the cold north and wish you would bring your bag south where it is warm, and teach students here."

Hahn Am wrote back, "I am very poor. I think about an old loan."

Man Gong answered, "The old man loved his grandson and his mouth is poor."

Hahn Am wrote, "The thief has already passed. Don't pull your bow."

Man Gong replied, "The arrow has already pierced the thief's head."

What is the meaning of:

1 ☺ "I am very poor. I think about an old loan?"

2 ☺ "The old man loved his grandson and his mouth is poor."

3 ☺ "The thief has already passed. Don't pull your bow."

4 ☺ "The arrow has already pierced the thief's head."

COMMENTARY

Two old men are pulling the arms of a young child, shouting, "That's my son!" "No, that's my son!" Letting go is better than holding.

The Great Way Has No Gate

A monk asked Zen Master Hyang Gok, "What is the meaning of 'The great way has no gate'?"

Hyang Gok replied, "Quiet, quiet speech."

The monk asked, "What is quiet, quiet speech?"

"In the east and west are ten million worlds. South, north, one million lands."

1. 🔘 What is the meaning of "The great way has no gate"?

2. 🔘 What is "quiet, quiet speech"?

3. 🔘 Are Hyang Gok's two answers correct or not?

COMMENTARY

Opening your mouth is already a mistake. You must use your legs.

Joju's Cypress Tree in the Garden

A monk asked Zen Master Hyang Gok, "What is the meaning of Joju's cypress tree in the garden?"

"Living in a strong tiger's mouth, falling into a blue dragon's cave."

🔘 What does Joju's cypress tree in the garden mean?

🔘 What does Hyang Gok's answer mean?

🔘 Can you live in a tiger's mouth?

103

COMMENTARY

Look! Look at the cypress tree in the garden. Then you will get it.

The Meaning of Joju's "Mu"

A monk asked, "What is the meaning of Joju's 'Mu'?"

Hyang Gok answered, "A demon falls down. Buddha runs away, scared and shaking."

1. ⊘ What does "Mu" mean?

2. ⊘ "A demon falls down. Buddha runs away, scared and shaking." What does this mean?

COMMENTARY

You must visit a dairy farm and listen carefully to the cow's song.

105

The Meaning of Dry Shit on a Stick

A monk asked Zen Master Hyang Gok, "What does Un Mun's 'Dry shit on a stick' mean?"

Hyang Gok answered, "The bright sun appears in the sky at midnight. Above heaven, below heaven, without equal."

1. What does Un Mun's "Dry shit on a stick" mean?
2. Is Hyang Gok's answer correct?
3. Did you see the bright sun appear in the sky at midnight?

Commentary

You must go to a farm and ask the farmer, "Where's the dry shit on a stick?"

106

The Meaning of Three Pounds of Flax

A monk asked Zen Master Hyang Gok, "What is the meaning of 'Three pounds of flax'?"

"The iron cow was surprised, ran away past the western sky and Sumi Mountain, then crossed the big river at midnight."

1. What is the meaning of "Three pounds of flax"?
2. How many percent correct is Hyang Gok's answer?

⊘ "The iron cow … crossed the big river at midnight."
What does this mean?

Commentary

Wake up! See clearly, hear clearly. One pound of iron
equals one pound of kapok.

Realm of Enlightenment

A monk asked Zen Master Hyang Gok, "What is your
realm of enlightenment?"

"The sun rising is Manjushri's house. The moon setting is
Kwan Seum Bosal's house."

⊘ What is your realm of enlightenment?
⊘ Are Manjushri's house and Kwan Seum Bosal's house
the same or different?

Commentary

In the morning, the sun rises in the east. In the evening,
the sun sets in the west.

107
上
下月

What Is Your Everyday Life?

When a monk asked Zen Master Hyang Gok, "What is your everyday life?" Hyang Gok answered, "Break the blue dragon's cave with an iron hammer. Change a golden-haired lion into a dig."

1. ⊘ What is your everyday life?
2. ⊘ Is Hyang Gok's answer correct or not?
3. ⊘ How do you break the blue dragon's cave and change the golden-haired lion into a dog?

COMMENTARY

When you are tired, sleep. When you are hungry, eat. When you meet someone, ask, "How are you today?"

Face of Fire in the Rocks

When someone asked Zen Master Hyang Gok, "What is Buddha?" he answered, "Face of fire in the rocks."

1. ⊘ What is Buddha?
2. ⊘ What is the meaning of "Face of fire in the rocks"?

COMMENTARY

The train goes down the tracks. The bus goes down the highway.

110

Face of Rocks in the Fire

When someone asked Zen Master Hyang Gok, "What is the eminent teacher?" he answered, "Face of rocks in the fire."

1 ☺ What is the eminent teacher?

2 ☺ What is the meaning of "Face of rocks in the fire"?

COMMENTARY

Hyang Gok's face is in heaven and his body is in hell.

111

Hyang Gok's "Bodhidharma's Coming to China"

When someone asked Zen Master Hyang Gok, "What is the meaning of Bodhidharma's coming to China?" he answered, "Make a mud horse in the fire."

1 ☺ What is the meaning of Bodhidharm's coming to China?

2 ☺ How do you make a mud horse in the fire?

COMMENTARY

Bodhidharma had two eyes, two ears, one mouth. Three years after he died he was alive again. See his body clearly. Hear his sound clearly.

Kong-An

Where All Buddhas Appear

Someone asked Zen Master Hyang Gok, "What is the place where all Buddhas appear?"

"Iron cow runs over a bridge of rabbit's horn," he responded.

1 ⊙ What is the place where all Buddhas appear?

2 ⊙ Did you see the rabbit's horn and the iron cow running?

Commentary

See clearly, hear clearly. Water is flowing, the wind is blowing.

What Is Meditation?

Someone asked Zen Master Hyang Gok, "What is meditation?"

"Not-moving form in the morning," he replied.

1 ⊙ What is meditation?

2 ⊙ What is "not-moving form in the morning"?

Commentary

Open your mouth and you will receive thirty blows.

114

Great Liberation

Someone asked Zen Master Hyang Gok, "What is great liberation?"

"Mud cow crossed a big river."

1. What is great liberation?
2. How does a mud cow cross a big river?

Commentary

If you are moving, you are already dead. If you are not moving, you instantly fall into the river of hell.

115

The Samadhi of Great Stillness

Someone asked Zen Master Hyang Gok, "What is the samadhi of great stillness?"

"A long time ago the golden bird flew into the North Star and still received no news," he replied.

1. What is the samadhi of great stillness?
2. What is the meaning of "no news"?

Commentary

Opening your mouth, you lose your tongue.

Clear Original Body

Once a student asked Zen Master Hyang Gok, "What is the clear original body?"

"The treasure sword is hidden in the Diamond Eyes," he answered.

1  What is the clear original body?

2 What is the meaning of "The treasure sword is hidden in the Diamond Eyes"?

3 What is the treasure sword?

COMMENTARY

In the morning, eat breakfast. At noon, eat lunch.

Pomegranate Feast

Bo Wol offered a ripe pomegranate to Zen Master Man Gong. As he was handing it to his teacher, he said, "Please eat this fruit in a feast with the Bodhisattvas of the ten directions and the Buddhas of the three worlds." Man Gong took the fruit, ate it, and smiled. "How is it?" Bo Wol asked.

"The Bodhisattvas of the ten directions and the Buddhas

of the three worlds have already finished the feast," Man Gong replied.

1   The Bodhisattvas of the ten directions and the Buddhas of the three worlds come from where?

2   How did Zen Master Man Gong feast with Bodhisattv

COMMENTARY

Monkeys like bananas. Horses like apples.

118

STONE KWAN SEUM BOSAL

Zen Master Man Gong, while standing in front of the stone Kwan Seum Bosal statue at Jeong Hae Sah Temple, said to his student, Bo Wol, "Describe Kwan Seum Bosal's face."

"Beneficent," was the reply. Upon hearing this, Man Gong returned to his room.

1   If you were Bo Wol, how would you answer?

2   Man Gong said nothing and returned to his room. What is the meaning of this action?

3   If you were Man Gong and Bo Wol gave you this answer, what would you do?

4 ⊘ Who was the winner and who was the loser?

COMMENTARY

Man Gong and Bo Wol are wrestling in a mud puddle. Who wins, who loses? The statue has a mouth but no speech. It has eyes but cannot see. When you hear the statue's speech, and the statue sees, then you are complete.

✗

IN the SouND of the Bell, AttaiN ENlightENMENt

Zen Master Seung Sahn's grandteacher, Man Gong, gave a Dharma speech to a group of monks: "All Zen Masters say that in the sound of the bell they attain enlightenment, and at the sound of the drum they fall down. Anyone who understands the meaning of this, please give me an answer."

A student named Song Wol stood up and said, "If the rabbit's horn is correct, the sheep's horn is false." Man Gong smiled.

⊘ "In the sound of the bell they attain enlightenment, and at the sound of the drum they fall down." What does this mean?

119 回

五

十二

- "If the rabbit's horn is correct, the sheep's horn is false." What does this mean?
- Was Man Gong's smile a reward or a punishment?

COMMENTARY

If you cannot hear the bell or the drum, you are free. If you hear both sounds you are already in hell.

The Great Work of Life and Death

Carrying rice paper and brush, Yong Um Sunim entered Zen Master Man Gong's room and said, "Master, please write down one sentence." Man Gong took the brush and wrote, "This is the realm of finishing the great work of life and death: At midnight on the mountain peak the monkey's cry is very noisy." Yong Um thanked Man Gong and kept this sentence his whole life. Later, Zen Master Kum Bong read the sentence and said, "Zen Master Man Gong's keen eyes and bone marrow are in this sentence."

- What is "the realm of finishing the great work of life and death"?

en

2 "At midnight on the mountain peak the monkey's cry very noisy." What does this mean?

3 What are Man Gong's keen eyes and bone marrow?

COMMENTARY

Speech and words are free. Action is a hindrance. So your mouth and body must have a good friendship.

Best Killer

One day, Hyo Bong Sunim asked Zen Master Man Gong, "Somebody likes to kill. Who is the best killer?"

Man Gong said, "Today I see him here."

"I want to cut your neck," Hyo Bong said. "Do you give me permission?"

Man Gong answered him. Then Hyo Bong was very happy and bowed to his teacher.

1 Who is the best killer?

2 Man Gong said, "Today I see him here." What does this mean?

3 What was Man Gong's second answer?

Kong-An

Be careful. Don't give a sharp knife to a child.

Big Temple

Zen Master Man Gong told the following story to Hyo Bong Sunim: "A long time ago, the Heaven King picked up a blade of grass and put it back into the ground. He then said to Shakyamuni Buddha, 'I made a big temple here.' The Buddha smiled.

"So, Hyo Bo Sunim, do you understand the meaning of this?"

Hyo Bong gave an answer to Zen Master Man Gong, who clapped his hands and, laughing, said, "Wonderful, wonderful!"

1. ⊘ "I have made a big temple here." What does this mean?
2. ⊘ What does the Buddha's smile mean?
3. ⊘ What was Hyo Bong Sunim's answer to Zen Master Man Gong?

Commentary

Everything is impermanent. Why make a temple? If you attain "Everything is impermanent," you attain the true temple.

Departure Poem

Ko Bong Sunim went into Zen Master Man Gong's room, bowed to his teacher, and said, "I will soon leave and travel around the country."

"If you are leaving, give me a departure poem," Man Gong said.

But Ko Bong only waved his hands in denial and said, "Today I am very busy. I cannot write a poem."

"I'll see you next time," his teacher said. "Have a good trip."

1. ⊙ If you had been there, what would your departure poem have been?

2. ⊙ Ko Bong waved his hands and said, "Today I am very busy. I cannot write a poem." Is that reply correct?

Commentary

Already everything is very clear: staying, coming and going. A beautiful poem is already in front of you.

Let's Drink Tea

Ko Bong Sunim went into Zen Master Man Gong's room and bowed to him.

Zen

"Welcome, Ko Bong. Let's drink some tea."

Ko Bong then helped Man Gong, bowed, and sat down. Man Gong was very happy.

1 ⊘ Man Gong said, "Let's drink some tea." At that time, what would you have done?

2 ⊘ How did Ko Bong help Man Gong?

COMMENTARY

Ko Bong has two hands. Man Gong has one mouth. Teatime and dinnertime have already passed. Open the door and go downtown.

125 Does an Enlightened Person Have Life and Death?

Kum Bong asked Zen Master Hae Wol, "If a person gets enlightenment, does that person have life and death?"

Hae Wol replied, "Do you see the sky? Does it appear or disappear?" Kum Bong couldn't answer. He then went to see Zen Master Man Gong and told him of his exchange with Hae Wol.

Man Gong said, "Why did you leave Zen Master Hae Wol

without answering him, and then come to me?"

"What could I have said?"

Man Gong replied, "Why do you check so much?" Kum Bong was stuck again. Then suddenly he attained, stood up and bowed to the Zen Master. Man Gong was very happy and said, "Wonderful, wonderful!"

1. Does an enlightened person have life and death?

2. Does the sky appear or disappear?

3. What did Kum Bong attain?

COMMENTARY

If you are thirsty, have a drink. If you are tired, sleep. The sky is always blue, and the mountain is forever green. The dog understands dog's job; the cat understands cat's job.

Wei Sahn's Cow

Zen Master Jun Kang once gave the following Dharma speech: "Everything has Buddha-nature. But Buddha-nature is originally empty. So how can everything have Buddha-nature?" The assembly of monks was silent.

He continued, "A long time ago, the famous Chinese Zen Master Wei Sahn said, 'When I die, I will be reborn a cow at my layman's house.'

"So my question is, what do you call him? Is he Wei Sahn or is he a cow?"

1  Everything has Buddha-nature. But Buddha-nature is originally empty. So how can everything have Buddha-nature?

2 When Wei Sahn dies, he becomes a cow: at that time, would you call him Zen Master Wei Sahn or a cow?

COMMENTARY

What do you see now? What do you hear now? Everything is clear in front of you.

127

Stone Buddha

Zen Master Man Gong was walking in the countryside with Sae Kyong Sunim, who saw a stone Buddha in the field and said to Man Gong, "I think that Buddha is very old. When was it made, Master?"

"Before the ancient Buddha appeared."

1 ⊘ What is stone Buddha?

2 ⊘ "Before the ancient Buddha appeared." What does this mean?

COMMENTARY

See clearly, hear clearly. The earth is round, the sky has no limits. If you meet a Buddha, offer incense and bow three times. If there is no Buddha, sit on the ground.

The Buddha's Breast

Hae Am Sunim was standing in front of a statue of the Buddha with Zen Master Man Gong, who said, "The Buddha's breast is very wonderful and big, so at this temple all the monks have enough food."

"If someone does not have good karma, how can they drink the Buddha's milk?"

Man Gong looked at Hae Am and said, "What did you say?"

"I said, 'If someone does not have good karma, how can they drink the Buddha's milk?'"

Man Gong replied, "You only touch the Buddha's breast, so you cannot drink the Buddha's milk."

- ⊘ How do you drink the Buddha's milk?
- ⊘ What is good karma?
- ⊘ Man Gong said, "You only touch the Buddha's breast, so you cannot drink the Buddha's milk." What does this mean?

COMMENTARY

My stomach is already full of milk.

Why Do You Cover Your Eyes?

One day Gum Oh Sunim visited Zen Master Man Gong. Upon entering the Master's room he said, "Nothing, nothing. Where is the great Zen Master?"

Man Gong asked, "Why do you cover your eyes?"

Again Gum Oh said, "Nothing, nothing. Where is the great Zen Master?"

Man Gong replied, "You are a liar who hangs around these parts."

Then Gum Oh said, "Master, be careful, be careful. Don't be deceived."

Man Gong smiled and laughed.

1 Ⓠ Gum Oh said, "Nothing, nothing. Where is the great Zen Master?" What does this mean?

2 Ⓠ Zen Master Man Gong replied, "Why do you cover your eyes?" What does this mean?

3 Ⓠ If somebody lies to you, what can you do?

COMMENTARY

Two blind men, wrestling each other, fall into the mud. How do they get out?

130

Hae Cho Asks About Buddha

Hae Cho asked Zen Master Poep An, "What is Buddha?"

"Hae Cho!"

"Yes?"

"That is Buddha," Poep An said.

1 Ⓠ What is Buddha?

2 Ⓠ Poep An said, "Hae Cho!" What does this mean?

3 Hae Cho replied, "Yes?" and Poep An said, "That is Buddha." What does this mean?

COMMENTARY

Hae Cho is Buddha, Buddha is Hae Cho. No Hae Cho, no Buddha. Hae Cho is Hae Cho, Buddha is Buddha. Which one do you like?

Why Bodhidharma Came to China

Dae Un Sunim said to Zen Master Man Gong, "Kwan Sahn No Sunim and I visited Zen Master Hahn Am. Kwan Sahn asked him, 'On the outside, this mountain is very dry, but inside it is not dry, so a lot of grass and trees grow on it—it is very strong. What does this mean?' Hahn Am answered by chomping his teeth together three times. I don't understand what this means, master. Please teach me."

"That has already passed," Man Gong said. "Hahn Am and Kwan Sahn No Sunim are no longer necessary. You must ask me your question."

"Why did Bodhidharma come to China?"

Man Gong replied, "A long time ago, Ananda asked Mahakashyapa, 'The Buddha transmitted to you the Golden Brocade Robe. What else did he transmit to you?' So, Mahakashyapa called out, 'Ananda!' 'Yes, sir?' 'Knock down the flagpole in front of the gate.' Dae Un Sunim, do you understand what this means? If you do, then you understand why Bodhidharma came to China."

Dae Un stood up and bowed to Man Gong, but the great Zen Master only laughed and said, "No, no. More practice is necessary."

1. Hahn Am chomped his teeth together three times. What does this mean?

2. "Bodhidharma came to China." What does this mean?

3. How do you knock down the flagpole in front of the gate?

4. Why did Man Gong laugh and say, "No, no. More practice is necessary"?

COMMENTARY

The American flag has many stars and stripes. The Japanese flag has a red sun. The South Korean flag has a yin-yang symbol.

Dragon's Nostrils

Zen Master Man Gong returned to Jeong Hae Sah from Oh Dae Sahn Stillness Palace Treasure Temple. Upon his arrival, Boek Cho Sunim asked him, "Master, at Oh Dae Sahn Stillness Palace Treasure Temple, there is a dragon. Did you see the dragon's nostrils or not?"

"Yes, I saw them."

"How big are they?"

Man Gong made a "hmhhh" sound.

◎   What are dragon's nostrils?

◎   Man Gong made a "hmhhh" sound. What does this mean?

COMMENTARY

The dragon's breath blew Man Gong and Boek Cho to heaven.

Everything Has Already Become Buddha

During a Dharma speech delivered from the high rostrum, Zen Master Man Gong had the following exchange with a student: "One sutra says, 'Everything has already become

Buddha.' Does anyone understand what this means?"

Jin Song Sunim answered, "Dirty water, two buckets."

Man Gong shouted, "How do you take care of dirty water?"

Jin Song shouted, "KATZ!"

Man Gong hit Jin Song on the head with his Zen stick.

Jin Song bowed to Man Gong and left.

Then Man Gong said, "The correct Zen Dharma eyes are not reckless."

1. "Everything has already become Buddha." What does this mean?
2. Why did Jin Song say "Dirty water, two buckets"?
3. Where is Jin Song's mistake?
4. What does Man Gong's "Zen Dharma eyes are not reckless" mean?

COMMENTARY

Grandson is crying. The grandmother is sad and gives him candy.

Candlelight

One evening, Zen Master Man Gong lit a candle by the window in his room. He then asked his attendant, "Which is the true light, the candlelight or the light reflected in the window?"

The attendant blew out the candle and said, "Master, what can you do?" Man Gong then re-lit the candle.

- ☉ Man Gong asked, "Which is the true light, the candle light or the light reflected in the window?" If you were the attendant, how would you have answered?

- ☉ Before Man Gong lit the candle, there was no light. Where did the light come from?

Commentary

No eyes, no light. No mouth, no speech. If you turn on the light, the room is bright. If you turn off the light, the room is dark.

Why Do You Bring Me Tea?

One day, while Zen Master Man Gong was sitting in his room and enjoying the view outside his window, his attendant brought him some tea. Man Gong said, "Every day I don't do

nything. Why do you bring me tea?"

His attendant leaned close to him and said, "Have another up, please."

Master Man Gong smiled.

🔘 "Every day I don't do anything." What does this mean?

🔘 If you were the attendant, how would you have answered Man Gong?

COMMENTARY

One mind appears, the whole world appears. One mind disppears, the whole world disappears. Don't check—just do it.

Our Temple Buddha Is White

One morning, during a particularly snowy winter, two nuns wept the snow from the road that ran between Kyun Song ım and Zen Master Man Gong's residence at nearby Jun Vol Sah Hermitage. When they reached his quarters, they owed to him and said, "Master, we have removed the snow rom the road. We invite you to have breakfast. Please come."

"I will not go on your clean road," he said.

en

One of the nuns asked, "Then what road will you take?"

"Your temple Buddha is white."

1 ◎ Man Gong said, "I will not go on your clean road." What does this mean?

2 ◎ "Your temple Buddha is white." What does this mean?

COMMENTARY

Two nuns killed Man Gong, but they still have mouths.

Mahakashyapa's Flag

One day Zen Master Man Gong gave a Dharma speech from the high rostrum. "Ananda asked Mahakashyapa, 'The Buddha transmitted the golden brocade robe to you. What else did he transmit to you?' Mahakashyapa called out, 'Ananda!' 'Yes, Sir!' 'Knock down the flagpole in front of the gate.' So I ask you, what else did the Buddha transmit? What is the meaning of this?"

At that time, the Head Nun Poep Hi Sunim called out, "Great Zen Master! Fish swimming, water is a little cloudy. Bird flying, feathers come off."

Then Boek Cho Sunim called out, "Zen Master! You are a great Master, so I cannot talk to you."

"Why can't you talk to me?"

"Great Master, you don't understand my speech."

Man Gong replied, "These ears are very old."

- ☯ Ananda asked Mahakashyapa, "What else did he transmit to you?" What does this mean?

- ☯ Poep Hi answered, "Fish swimming, water is a little cloudy. Bird flying, feathers come off." What does this mean?

- ☯ Boek Cho said, "You are a great Master, so I cannot talk to you." What does this mean?

- ☯ What does Boek Cho's second answer, "Great Master, you don't understand my speech" mean?

- ☯ Man Gong replied, "These ears are very old." What does this mean?

COMMENTARY

Three people start fighting in a boat and the boat capsizes. Then they yell, "Help! Help!"

138

The Complete Stillness

One day Zen Master Man Gong received a letter from Ha
In Sah Temple. The monks asked, "In the ten directions,
numberless temples are made in the Complete Stillness Jewe
Palace. We are not clear about this. So we ask you, Master,
where is the Complete Stillness Jewel Palace?"

Man Gong wrote them this poem:

> *In the ten directions,*
> *Numberless temples*
> *are in the Complete Stillness Jewel Palace.*
> *This palace is built in my nostril.*

They wrote back to Man Gong and said, "You say the
Complete Stillness Jewel Palace is built in your nostril. We
want you to guide us to the Complete Stillness Jewel Palace."

Man Gong replied, "Why don't you know? You already sta
in the Complete Stillness Jewel Palace at Hae In Sah Temple
in Ka Ya Sahn."

1 ◯ Where is the Complete Stillness Jewel Palace?

2 ◯ Man Gong said, "This palace is built in my nostril."
What does this mean?

3 ◯ What does Man Gong's second answer, "You already

tay in the Complete Stillness Jewel Palace in Hae In Sah
Temple in Ka Ya Sahn" mean?

COMMENTARY

This nose comes from where? Who made this nose?
Originally there is no nose. How does a temple appear?

The Buddha Saw a Star

Zen Master Man Gong received a letter on Buddha's
Enlightenment Day, in which the monks of Kung Dong Zen
Temple asked him, "On December 8 in the early morning the
Buddha saw a star and got Enlightenment. What does this mean?"

Man Gong wrote back, "The Buddha saw a star and said
he got Enlightenment. This is sand falling into the eyes."

1 ⊘ "The Buddha saw a star and got Enlightenment."
   What does this mean?

2 ⊘ What kind of star did the Buddha see when he got
   Enlightenment?

3 ⊘ "This is sand falling into the eyes." What does this mean?

Does this star come from your mind, your eyes, or the sky? If you attain this point, you attain your true self.

Cannot Get Out

Layman Sok Du made a circle on the ground, pointed to it and asked Zen Master Man Gong, "Master, all the great monks in the world cannot go in. Why?"

Man Gong replied, "All the great monks in the world cannot get out of it."

1. ◎ Layman Sok Du made a circle. What does this mean?
2. ◎ Why can't all the great monks go into the circle?
3. ◎ Man Gong replied, "All the great monks in the world cannot get out of it." What does this mean?

COMMENTARY

Don't make anything. Open your mouth and you go straight to hell like an arrow. Close your mouth and you have already lost your life. You must perceive that.

141

Rat New Year

For the Rat New Year, a layman sent a letter to Zen Master Man Gong which said, "Everybody says, 'Old year going, new year coming.' I don't understand. Old year and new year, what does that mean?"

"This is Rat New Year," Man Gong replied.

1. Old year going, new year coming. Coming from where? Going where?
2. What is old year? What is new year?
3. What is Rat New Year?

COMMENTARY

The rabbit's ears are long and its tail is short.

142

Heaven and Earth Are Separate

When Zen Master Seung Sahn's grandteacher, Zen Master Mang Gong, was staying at Kum Sun Hermitage in Jeong Hae Sah Temple, Zen Master Hae Bong visited him and said, "There's an old saying, 'In the true, even if there is one hair's breadth, heaven and earth are separate.'"

Kong-Ans

Mang Gong replied, "Even if there is no hair's breadth, heaven and earth are separate."

1 ⊘ "Even if there is one hair's breadth, heaven and earth are separate." What does this mean?

2 ⊘ "Even if there is not one hair's breadth, heaven and earth are separate." What does this mean?

3 ⊘ What is the difference between one hair's breadth and not one hair's breadth?

Commentary

If you open your mouth, it's a mistake. If you keep your mouth closed, then that, too, is a mistake. Without an open or closed mouth, just see, just hear.

Understand Your Job

One day, as Zen Master Man Gong was giving a Dharma speech from the high rostrum, Zen Master Hae Bong opened the door to the room and came in. Man Gong interrupted the speech to say, "Now the great tiger is coming in."

Immediately, Hae Bong took a tiger's form and roared,

"Rrrrwww!"

Man Gong said, "He understands his job. Only go straight.

1 ◎ Why did Zen Master Man Gong say "Now the great tiger is coming in"?

2 ◎ Why did Zen Master Hae Bong take a tiger's form and roar?

3 ◎ What is your original job?

COMMENTARY

A tiger understands a tiger. A dog understands a dog.

144 Space Also Becomes Old

One summertime Zen Master Man Gong visited Zen Master Yong Song in Seoul. As they sat facing each other, Yong Song said, "Man Gong, you have become old."

"Space also becomes old," Man Gong replied. "Why wouldn't this form-body become old?"

1 ◎ No life, no death. How do you become old?

2 ◎ "Space also becomes old." What does this mean?

3 ◎ If you say Dharma-body and form-body are the same,

hen Dharma-body also becomes old. If you say they are different, those two bodies come from where?

COMMENTARY

Form is emptiness, emptiness is form. No form, no emptiness. Form is form, emptiness is emptiness.

Happy New Year

While staying at Nae Jang Sah Temple, Zen Master Sol Bong sent a New Year's card to Zen Master Man Gong. In the card he asked, "How do you take one more step from the top of a hundred-foot pole?"

Man Gong answered, "KATZ! Happy New Year!"

1 ⊙ How do you take one more step from the top of a hundred-foot pole?

2 ⊙ "KATZ! Happy New Year!" What does this mean?

COMMENTARY

Aigo! Aigo! Aigo!

Hold Up One Finger

One day, Zen Master Sol Bong visited Kum Sun Hermitage in Jeong Hae Sah Temple and asked Zen Master Man Gong, "The Buddha held up a flower. What does this mean?"

Man Gong held up one finger.

Sol Bong bowed to him.

"What did you attain?" Man Gong asked.

Sol Bong replied, "A second offense is not permitted."

- ⊘ The Buddha held up a flower. What does this mean?
- ⊘ Man Gong held up one finger. What does this mean?
- ⊘ What did Sol Bong attain?
- ⊘ Why did Sol Bong say, "A second offense is not permitted"?

COMMENTARY

Mistake, mistake, mistake. Flower and finger are very clear. The flower is the flower, the finger is the finger.

Peop Ki Bosal's Grass

After a visit to Diamond Mountain in what is now North Korea, Zen Master Man Gong returned to Jeong Hae Sah

Temple and gave a Dharma speech: "When I went to Diamond Mountain, I heard about Poep Ki Bosal, so I went to listen to her give a speech. She said, 'Students, do you understand why grass grows up three inches?'" Pausing for a moment, Man Gong asked the assembly of monks, "Do you understand the true meaning of this?" Nobody could answer him.

Later, one of the students asked Man Gong, "Poep Ki Bosal said, 'Grass grows up three inches.' What does this mean?"

Man Gong replied, "Don't ask me about grass growing up. You must go out into the grass, and then you will understand Buddha's obligation."

The student asked, "How do I go out into the grass?"

Man Gong said, "Walking at night is not permitted. Come ask me tomorrow."

1. ☯ "Grass grows up three inches." What does this mean?
2. ☯ "Grass grows up" and "into the grass" — are they the same or different?
3. ☯ "Walking at night is not permitted. Come ask me tomorrow." What does this mean?

Stupid, stupid, stupid. If you find Poep Ki Bosal's mouth,
en you will understand.

ak Myong's Five Questions

Zen Master Hak Myong of Nae Jang Sah Temple sent five
estions to all the Zen Temples in Korea. The questions were:

1. Snow comes down and completely fills the valley.
   Why is there only one pine tree still standing there?
2. The whole world is Vairocana Buddha's body. Where
   can you find your true self?
3. All rivers flow into the ocean. Where can you taste
   fresh water?
4. Before becoming a cicada, broken caterpillar. At that
   time, not cicada, not caterpillar: What do you call it?
5. In this world, everyone has many close friends. Who
   is the closest?

Zen Master Man Gong answered him, "Too much think-
g. I give you thirty blows. This stick—what do you call it?"

148

生
死
崖
頭

1 ⊘ How do you answer the five questions, one by one?

2 ⊘ Man Gong said, "Too much thinking. I give you thirty blows." Is that correct or not?

3 ⊘ Man Gong asked, "This stick—what do you call it?" So, I ask you, what do you call it?

COMMENTARY

Five entrances into one room.

149

Three Zen Masters' "KATZ!"

One day Zen Master Hae Wol invited Zen Master Man Gong to Tong Do Sah Temple. Lunch was served and everyone was about to begin, when suddenly Hae Wol shouted "KATZ!" Everyone was very surprised, but the Head Monk simply hit the chukpi, so they all began eating. At the end of the meal, just before the chukpi was hit again, Man Gong shouted "KATZ!" Everyone was startled, but the Head Monk just hit the chukpi three times and the meal was over.

Later, monks from all the Zen temples began talking about the two Zen Masters' "KATZ": "Which one is correct?" "Are they the same or different?" "What do they mean?" Finally, one monk asked Zen Master Yong Song, "What is the meaning of the two Zen Masters' 'KATZ!'?"

Yong Song replied, "I don't like to open my mouth, but because everybody wants to know what this means, I will teach you."

Then Yong Song shouted, "KATZ!"

1 ☺ What does Hae Wol's "KATZ!" mean?
2 ☺ What does Man Gong's "KATZ!" mean?
3 ☺ Are the three Zen Masters' "KATZ!" the same or different?

COMMENTARY

If you attain "KATZ!" you understand Man Gong's mouth and Hae Wol's ears.

MIND LIGHT   *Poem by Zen Master Kyong Ho*

Moments before he died, Zen Master Kyong Ho wrote the following poem:

150

The mind moon is very bright and round —
Its light swallows everything.
When both mind and light disappear,
What … is …this …?

1. "The mind moon is very bright and round?" What does this mean?

2. How can light swallow everything?

3. "Mind and light disappear"—then what?

Commentary

Don't make anything. What do you see now? What do you hear now? When you are doing something, just do it.

The Tree With No Shadows   *Poem by Zen Master Kyong Ho*

That's funny—
Riding a cow, wanting to find a cow
When you find the tree with no shadow,
The ocean's waves all disappear.

1. "That's funny—riding a cow, wanting to find a cow." What does this mean?

2. Where is the tree with no shadow?

151

3 ⊙   "The ocean's waves all disappear." Then what?

COMMENTARY

Wake up! The mountain is blue, the water is flowing—
Dol, dol, dol.

Zen Master Man Gong's Poem for His Teacher, Zen Master Kyong Ho*

> *Empty mirror is originally no mirror.*
> *Wake-up cow, there is no cow,*
> *No place, no road.*
> *Open eyes: drink and sex.*

1 ⊙   "Originally no mirror." Then what?

2 ⊙   "Wake-up cow, there is no cow." Then what?

3 ⊙   "No place, no road." Where do you stay?

4 ⊙   "Open eyes: drink and sex." What does this mean?

COMMENTARY

Everything is free: eyes, ears, nose, tongue, body, mind.
That is a great man.

* Kyong Ho means "empty mirror."

Zen Master Man Gong's Enlightenment Poem

When Zen Master Man Gong attained enlightenment, at the age of twenty-six, he composed the following poem:

Empty mountain, true energy without time and space.
White cloud and clear wind come and go by themselves.
Why did Bodhidharma come to China?
Rooster crowing in the morning,
Sun rising in the east.

153

1. What is the meaning of "Empty mountain, true energy without time and space"?

2. Why did Bodhidharma come to China?

3. Why is the rooster crowing at 3 am, the sun rising at 7 am?

Commentary

Silence is better than holiness. If you are tired, go to your room and sleep.

Zen Master Man Gong's Portrait Poem

I never leave you,
You never leave me.

154

Before "you" and "I" appear,
What is this?

1 ⊙ Who is first, you or me?

2 ⊙ Before "you" and "I" appear, what?

3 ⊙ Is Zen Master Man Gong inside or outside his portrait

COMMENTARY

Before words, what is your original face? He is your clear mirror

155

POEM at BLue Ocean   *by Zen Master Man Gong*

A man swallowed and spit out the whole world.
Passing blue ocean—there hides body and dragon's horn.
Diamond Poep Ki Bosal's body punctures the sky.
Vast blue ocean—ancient Buddha's mind.

1 ⊙ "A man swallowed and spit out the whole world."
What does this mean?

2 ⊙ "Vast blue ocean—ancient Buddha's mind." What
does this mean?

COMMENTARY

Stone cat is barking; ice snake pierces the diamond eyes.

Poem for a Student, Hae Il*   *by Zen Master Man Gong*

> *Wisdom sun makes the sky become red.*
> *Mind moon is always white.*
> *Red and white never end.*
> *Everything—great peace in spring.*

1 What is wisdom sun?

2 What is mind moon?

3 "Everything—great peace in spring." What does that mean?

Commentary

Spring has flowers, in winter there is snow. The sun shines during the day, and at night the moon is bright.

Poem for White Cloud   *by Zen Master Man Gong*

> *Don't say white cloud is a no-mind guest.*
> *The old monk forgets everything.*
> *But white cloud, why are you not my friend?*
> *Far away a chicken is crowing, then find myself.*

1 "The old monk forgets everything." Then what?

2 Are you and the white cloud the same or different?

Hae Il means "wisdom sun."

3 ☺ "Far away a chicken is crowing, then find myself."
What does this mean?

COMMENTARY

The stone dog is barking. The ice fish is afraid and runs away.

POEM FOR Pal GONG Sah Temple   *by Zen Master Man Gong*

> *After night, rain comes.*
> *10,000 Buddhas don't understand that.*
> *Don't know and don't know.*
> *When you hear the bell ring, attain go-away.*

1 ☺ "10,000 Buddhas don't understand that." What does
this mean?

2 ☺ "Don't know and don't know." What does this mean?

3 ☺ "When you hear the bell ring, attain go-away." What
did you attain?

COMMENTARY

The bell rings, "Ding, ding." All the monks take their robes
into the Dharma room.

159

Poem for Buddha's Enlightenment Day
by Zen Master Man Gong

> *The Buddha saw a star, got enlightenment.*
> *Man Gong saw a star, lost enlightenment.*
> *December 8th KATZ! explodes "got" and "lost."*
> *In the snow, plum flowers one-by-one are red.*

1 🟢 "The Buddha saw a star, got enlightenment. Man Gong saw a star, lost enlightenment"—are they the same or different?

2 🟢 "December 8th KATZ! explodes 'got' and 'lost'" What does this mean?

3 🟢 "In the snow, plum flowers one-by-one are red." What does this mean?

Commentary

Many stars in the sky. If you attain the Buddha's star, you will attain, "In the snow, plum flowers one-by-one are red."

❧

Poem for Kan Wol Do Island   *by Zen Master Man Gong*

> *The man who is not close to the Buddha and eminent teachers—*

> *Why does he make good friends with the blue ocean?*
> *He is an original natural man,*
> *So he stays in the natural.*

○ Why is the man not close to the Buddha and eminent teachers?

○ Who is he?

○ "He is an original natural man." What does this mean?

COMMENTARY

Originally there is nothing. The Buddha and the original natural man come from where? If you want to understand the meaning of this, look at the palm of your hand.

POEM FOR BUDDHA'S BIRTHDAY   *by Zen Master Man Gong*

> *Very tired, so the dream is very complicated:*
> *This morning a bird gave a Dharma speech to me.*
> *Today is Tiger Year's Buddha's Birthday.*
> *One hundred grasses understand themselves: yellow and red.*

○ "This morning a bird gave a Dharma speech to me." What does this mean?

2 How do "One hundred grasses understand themselves: yellow and red"?

3 Originally nothing—so how does Buddha's birthday appear?

COMMENTARY

Put it all down. What do you see now? What do you hear now

162

Vairocana Peak* *by Zen Master Man Gong, Autumn, 1925.*

Man climbing up the blue sky.
The top of Vairocana is very bright —
A seal on the Eastern Ocean.

1 How do you climb up the blue sky?

2 "The top of Vairocana is very bright." What does this mean?

3 If you have no Eastern Ocean, where is the seal?

COMMENTARY

South Mountain is the body, North Ocean is the face. Walking in the sky, playing with the stars.

* Highest Peak

Poem for Tae Hwa Sahn Mountain

by Zen Master Man Gong

> On the bones of the Great Mountain,
> flowing water cleans the ancient Buddha's mind.
> Do you understand the true meaning of this?
> You must ask the pine tree.

🍃 How is the ancient Buddha's mind cleaned?

🍃 "You must ask the pine tree." What did the pine tree say?

Commentary

The road is very old. The man walking on it is very young, holding the pine tree and laughing.

Another Poem for Tae Hwa Sahn Mountain

by Zen Master Man Gong

> Cloud and mountain have no same or different—
> That is the nothingness natural tradition.
> If you get the nothingness seal,
> Then you understand why the mountain is blue.

🍃 "Cloud and mountain have no same or different."
What does this mean?

- Did you attain the nothingness seal?
- Why is the mountain blue?

COMMENTARY

Originally there is nothing. Where do the sky, the ground, the mountains, and the rivers come from? If you open your mouth, everything appears.

Kyol Che Poem

Zen Master Man Gong

> When Kyol Che begins, the stone girl has a dream.
> When Kyol Che ends, the wooden man sings a song.
> Dream and song, put it all down.
> Look at the moon, bright as dark ink.

- What is the meaning of the stone girl's dream?
- "Dream and song, put it all down." How do you do this?
- What is the meaning of "The moon, bright as dark ink"?

COMMENTARY

The mud cow flies to the moon. The moon says, "Ah, my stomach is very happy!"

166

Poem for a Student, Bo Wol *by Zen Master Man Gong*

> *Form is emptiness; emptiness is also emptiness.*
> *Throw them both away.*
> *Then what is this?*
> *In wintertime, much ice.*

1 ☯ Form and emptiness—"throw them both away."
Then what?

2 ☯ "In wintertime, much ice." What does this mean?

Commentary

Before you were born, you had no eyes, no ears, and no mouth. What do you call this? Understand that and hear universal sound.

167

Poem for Zen Master Un An* *by Zen Master Man Gong*

> *Cloud appears, but never appears.*
> *When it disappears, it also never disappears.*
> *The place of never-appearing and never-disappearing;*
> *Cloud rocks: spring without time.*

* Un An means "cloud rocks."

Kong-An

- Where is the place of never-appearing and never-disappearing?
- "Cloud rocks: spring without time." What does this mean?

Commentary

Open your mouth and everything appears; close your mouth and everything disappears. If you have no mouth, you re already complete.

Poem for a Bamboo Fan   *by Zen Master Man Gong*

168

> *The paper is not paper, the bamboo is not bamboo.*
> *Clear wind comes from where?*
> *The place without paper and bamboo.*
> *Clear wind itself coming and going.*

- "The place without paper and bamboo." What does this mean?
- How does clear wind come and go?

Commentary

Is the wind from the fan or the paper? Don't check—only moving. Ah, wonderful!

169

Pranja Ship *by Zen Master Man Gong*

> *Everything is impermanent, but there is truth.*
> *You and I are not two, not one:*
> *Only your stupid thinking is nonstop.*
> *Already alive in the Prajna ship.*

1 ☯ "Everything is impermanent, but there is truth." What does this mean?

2 ☯ "You and I are two, not one." What does this mean?

3 ☯ "Already alive in the Pranja ship." What does this mean?

COMMENTARY

What do you see now, what do you hear now? Everything appears clearly in front of you.

170

Three Thousand KATZes *by Zen Master Man Gong*

> *Stepping to, stepping fro, what is this?*
> *Falling down in the field, that is Vairocana Buddha.*
> *Sometimes spit out, sometimes swallow heaven and earth.*
> *Standing on Dok Sahn Mountain, three thousand KATZes.*

1 ☯ What is stepping to and stepping fro?

Kong-An

2 ◎ How do you spit out and swallow heaven and earth?

3 ◎ What is the meaning of three thousand KATZes?

COMMENTARY

No eyes, no ears, no nose, no tongue, no body, no mind.
But everything is standing right in front of you.

Bo Dok Cave   *by Zen Master Man Gong*

> *Walking all day with a bamboo stick,*
> *I quickly reach the front of Bo Dok cave.*
> *Who is host, who is guest? They cannot see each other.*
> *Only very close by, the gurgle of the stream.*

1 ◎ Why can't host and guest see each other?

2 ◎ How do you get close to the gurgle of the stream?

COMMENTARY

The sound of the stream takes away both guest and host.

OUR SEASONS   *Poem by Zen Master Seung Sahn*

> *Flowers in the spring,*
> *In the summer, cool breezes.*
> *Leaves in the fall,*
> *In winter, pure snow.*
> *Is the world throwing me away?*
> *Am I throwing away the world?*
> *I lie in the Dharma room.*
> *I don't care about anything.*
> *White clouds floating in the sky,*
> *Clear water flowing down the mountain,*
> *The wind through the pagoda:*
> *I surrender my whole life to them.*

⊘ Who made the four seasons?

⊘ This world and you, are they the same or different?

⊘ How do you surrender your whole life to the clouds,
water, and wind?

COMMENTARY

The turning earth revolves around the sun, making the four
seasons. If there were no sun, the four seasons would never
appear. If you have no mind, you have no earth or sun. Are

en

there four seasons then? Put it down, put it down! If you have
nothing, lie down, only sleep.

173

ENLIGHTENMENT DAY POEM   *by Zen Master Man Gong*

> *In the sky, many stars.*
> *Which star did the Budddha see?*
> *Facing south, find the North Star.*
> *That is the Buddha's enlightenment star.*

1 ☯ Which is the Buddha's enlightenment star?

2 ☯ How can you find the North Star while facing south?

3 ☯ How big is the Buddha's enlightenment star?

COMMENTARY

Big mistake, big mistake. Put enlightenment down.

174

TRANSMISSION POEM FOR KO BONG*

by Zen Master Man Gong

> *The ancient Buddha never gave transmission.*

---

* Ko Bong means "old peak." Seung Sahn is the name of the high mountain in
China where the Seventh Patriarch lived and practiced.

> *How can I give transmission to you?*
> *The cloud disappears, the moon by itself is bright.*
> *Seung Sahn is Ko Bong.*

1. ☯ "The ancient Buddha never gave transmission." What does this mean?

2. ☯ "The cloud disappears, the moon by itself is bright." Then what?

3. ☯ Seung Sahn and Ko Bong—are they the same or different?

COMMENTARY

Form is emptiness, emptiness is form. Is the moonlight form or emptiness? Its face is very bright and beautiful.

Zen Master Seung Sahn's Enlightenment Poem

When Zen Master Seung Sahn was a young man, he went to Won Gak Sahn Mountain and did a one hundred-day solo retreat. During this retreat, he chanted the Great Dharani of Original Mind Energy continuously for twenty hours every day, and lived on a diet of crushed pine needles. After one hundred days, Seung Sahn attained enlightenment and composed the following poem:

観
音
見

175

The road at the bottom of Won Gak Sahn Mountain
is not the present road.
The man climbing with his backpack
is not a man of the past.
Tok, tok — his footsteps
transfix past and present.
Crows out of a tree.
Caw, caw, caw.

Soon afterward, Zen Master Seung Sahn was given formal Dharma Transmission by Zen Master Ko Bong.

1. At the moment of his enlightenment, what did Zen Master Seung Sahn attain?
2. "Tok, tok — his footsteps transfix past and present." What does this mean?
3. "Crows out of a tree — Caw, caw, caw." What does this mean?
4. What did Seung Sahn get from Zen Master Ko Bong?

COMMENTARY

Holy people understand holy people. Crazy people understand each other. What do you understand? It's already clear in front of you.

Zen Master Seung Sahn's Poem for Children

Children's Buddhist Sunday School
Hwa Gye Sah Temple, Seoul, 1981

> Your mind is Buddha,
> My mind is Buddha.
> Buddha looks at Buddha,
> Mind disappears.
> Pine tree shadow reflected on the pond
> is never wet.
> When pebbles are thrown into the water,
> The pine tree is dancing.

1. Mind and Buddha, are they the same or different?
2. "Mind disappears." Where did it go?
3. "Pine tree is dancing." What does this mean?

Commentary

Clear mind, clear Buddha. No mind, no Buddha. But no mind is true Buddha. Which one is correct? Opening your mouth is already a big mistake. Children throw rocks into the pond. The pine tree is dancing.

176

空
超
時
空

Original Face   Poem by Zen Master Seung Sahn

> *Your true self is always*
> *shining and free.*
> *Human beings make something*
> *and enter the ocean of suffering.*
> *Only without thinking*
> *can you return to your true self.*
> *The high mountain is always blue.*
> *White clouds coming, going.*

1. "Your true self is always shining." What does this mean?
2. How can you return to your true self?
3. Why are the clouds white and the mountain blue?

COMMENTARY

Follow speech, lose your life. Follow meaning, go to hell. Open your eyes—what do your see now? What do you hear now? Original face and truth already appear in front of you.

Hae Jae Poem, Shin Won Sah Temple, 1989

Poem by Zen Master Seung Sahn

> *Blue mountain, water flowing*

For one thousand years.
Stone's peak whiteness
For numberless kalpas.
If you attain original Hae Jae,
Ten thousand mountains and valleys,
Only blue.

1. When did color and time appear?
2. What is original Hae Jae?
3. When did the mountains and valleys separate?

COMMENTARY

The sky is my father, and ground is my mother. Mountain and water are my brother and sister. Clouds coming and going are my friends. My parents, my family, and my friends all have the same root. If you attain this root, everything is yours.

No Distinction   *Poem by Zen Master Seung Sahn*

Eyes see without seeing,
So no distinction.
Ears hear, but there's no sound,
so no good or bad.

Kong-An

No distinction, no good or bad.
Put everything down.
The blue mountain is complete stillness.
Moonlight shining everywhere.

1 ☉ What does "no distinction" mean?
2 ☉ No good or bad, then what?
3 ☉ Why put everything down?
4 ☉ "The blue mountain is complete stillness." How does
the moonlight shine everywhere?

Commentary

Eyes, ears, color, and sound are originally nothing. When
did they appear? If you find that "when," you can attain your
original face. If you cannot attain your original face, ask the
stone girl. Rain falling down, the stone girl's dress is wet.

Enlightenment Poem   *Poem by Zen Master Hahn Am*

Making rice over the fire, a great awakening.
The Lord of ancient Buddhas appears very clearly.
If somebody asks me why Bodhidharma came to China,
Under the rocks, flowing water-sound is never wet.

1   What did the Zen Master Hahn Am attain?

2   What is the meaning of "flowing water-sound is never wet"?

COMMENTARY

The blue mountain is always blue. The big rocks never move.

North Mountain, South Mountain

Poem by Zen Master Hahn Am

> *Underfoot there is sky, overhead there is ground.*
> *Originally there is no inside, no outside, no middle.*
> *A person without legs is walking. A person without*
>   *eyes sees something.*
> *North Mountain keeps silence, facing South Mountain.*

1   What is the meaning of lines one, two, and three?

2   "North Mountain keeps silence, facing South Mountain." Then what?

COMMENTARY

Ask the North Mountain and the South Mountain. They will give you a good answer.

Kong-Ans

182

Mind Moonlight *Poem by Zen Master Hahn Am*

> *Hear the dog barking and understand: guest coming.*
> *The crow's caw disconcerts people.*
> *Mind moonlight never changes for ten thousand years.*
> *One morning the wind comes and cleans our yard.*

What is the meaning of:

1. ☯ "Hear the dog barking and understand: guest coming.'
2. ☯ "Mind moonlight never changes for ten thousand years
3. ☯ "One morning the wind comes and cleans our yard."

COMMENTARY

If you see clearly and hear clearly, then everything appears clearly. But one thing has never appeared in front of you.

183

The Ten Thousand Samadhis Are Not Necessary

Poem by Zen Master Hahn Am

> *Deep pine tree valley:*
> *Sitting quietly,*
> *The moon was bright last night.*
> *The ten thousand samadhis are not necessary.*

Kong-An

When thirsty, drink.
When tired, sleep.

⊙ Why aren't the ten thousand samadhis necessary?

⊙ "When thirsty, drink. When tired, sleep." Why is meditation necessary?

COMMENTARY

Rockheads understand rockheads. Clever heads understand each other.

PEACH FLOWERS TURN PINK   *Poem by Zen Master Yong Song*

The Buddha and eminent teachers originally don't understand.
I also don't understand.
Only spring comes and peach flowers turn pink.
Clear wind is blowing from the mountain.

⊙ If the Buddha and eminent teachers don't understand, and if Zen Master Yong Song doesn't understand, how can he say that spring comes and peach flowers turn pink?

⊙ "Clear wind is blowing from the mountain." Then what?

Silence is better than speech.

Zen Master So Sahn's Enlightenment Poem

185

Sitting quietly, only go straight for ten years.
Deep in the mountains, the birds are never afraid.
Last night, hard rain in the pine trees near the pond.
Horn appears on a fish head,
The crane cries three times.

1 ◎ What did Zen Master So Sahn attain?

2 ◎ "Horn appears on a fish head, the crane cries three times." What does this mean?

Commentary

Use turtle hair to make a sweater. When the freezing wind blows, you will never be cold.

Moon and Wind   *Poem by Zen Master So Sahn*

> *River wind is flowing for 10,000 days.*
> *Mountain moon is shining for 10,000 nights.*
> *10,000 days and 10,000 nights of guests.*
> *How many times standing on the porch with wind and moon?*

⊙ What is "10,000 days and 10,000 nights of guests"?

⊙ How many times have you stood on the porch with the
   wind and moon?

Commentary

Facing the moon, the dog barks, "Woof, woof."

No White, No Blue   *Poem by Zen Master Hyo Bong*

> *Every day, human beings get older.*
> *Every year, the mountain is blue.*
> *Forget both human beings and the mountain—*
> *Then there's no white, no blue.*

⊙ How do you forget both human beings and the mountain?

⊙ No white, no blue. Then what?

186

187

COMMENTARY

When you open your mouth, everything appears and disappears. When you close your mouth, nothing appears or disappears. But if you have no mouth, you become Buddha.

The Ship with No Bottom   *Poem by Zen Master Hyo Bong*

188

If you want to take away the I-my-me mountain,
You must get a cane made out of rabbit horn.
If you want to cross the ocean of suffering,
You must take the ship with no bottom.

Where do you get a cane made of rabbit horn?

Where is the ship with no bottom?

COMMENTARY

Opening your mouth cannot save you from hell. Close your mouth and lose your life.

189

Plum Flowers Fly in the Snow

Dharma Master Hahn Yong Un recited his enlightenment poem to Zen Master Man Gong:

> *How many people stay in a worrying dream?*
> *The great one's original home is everywhere.*
> *One KATZ! sound breaks the whole world.*
> *Plum flowers fly in the snow.*

Man Gong replied, "Plum flowers fly in the snow. Where do they come down?"

"Turtle hair and rabbit's horn."

Man Gong laughed loudly, "Ha, ha, ha!" and asked the assembly, "What does that mean?"

One great nun, Poep Hi Sunim, came forward and said, "Snow melts, then ground appears."

"You've attained ground," Man Gong replied.

1. Where is a great one's original home?
2. "Plum flowers fly in the snow." What does that mean?
3. Man Gong asked where the plum flowers come down. How would you answer?
4. What is turtle hair and rabbit's horn?
5. "You've attained ground." What does that mean?

Wake up, wake up! Snow is white, the ground is brown.

Old Monk's Stick

Zen Master In Gak wrote a poem:

> *A long time ago, the Buddha stayed at Yong*
> *Sahn Mountain and held up a flower.*
> *Only Mahakashyapa smiled.*

One Zen Master commented: "This morning this old monk picks up a Zen stick. All gods and demons in the whole world are laughing!"

1. Are the Buddha's flower and Mahakashyapa's smile the same or different?
2. Why, when the old monk picked up his Zen stick, did all the gods and demons laugh?

COMMENTARY

Be careful, be careful! Look at something and lose your heart.

191

Good Time   *Poem by Zen Master Kyong Bong*

> *Mountain is quiet,*
> *Water is flowing,*
> *Moon is bright,*
> *Flower is blooming.*
> *At midnight, a good smell fills the world.*
> *A good time to drink tea.*

1 ⊘ What do you attain from this poem?

2 ⊘ What is a good time?

COMMENTARY

Children like candy; the old man likes noodles.

192

This World Is Complicated   *Poem by Zen Master Kyong Bong*

> *Cold wind, eyes like jewels;*
> *In the snow, a strong scent of plum flowers.*
> *There are many problems in this world, so it is very complicated.*
> *But if you truly understand what this means,*
> *Then you understand the correct way.*

1 ⊘ Everything is complete. Why are there so many problems

Kong-Ans

in this world and why is everything so complicated?

2 ◯ If you truly understand the meaning of the first two
lines, then how do you understand the correct way?

COMMENTARY

With no eyes, no ears, no nose, no tongue, and no body,
everything appears clearly.

LAUGHING SOUNDS   *Poem by Zen Master Jun Kang*

Zen Master Jun Kang recited a poem to the assembly:

When you truly see this world, everything is just like this.
If your eyes are like Bodhidharma's,
Then there is much laughing and dancing!
The moon is bright in the sky;
The sun and stars are very quiet—
Only sounds of laughing fill the valley.

Then he commented, "Everybody heard these laughing
sounds and got enlightenment."

◯ What are eyes like Bodhidharma's?

◯ Why, if you have eyes like Bodhidharma's, is there

193 石女羅又舞

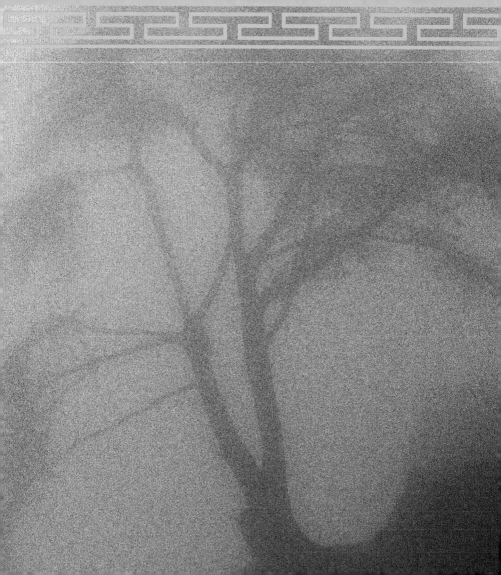

laughing and dancing?

- Did you hear the laughing sounds fill the valley?

A great thief! Watch your pockets!!

The Clear, Mystic Thing

Zen Master Man Gong sat on a high stand to give a Dharma speech, declaring, "Originally the six roots, six dusts, and six consciousnesses are empty, but one clear mystic thing made everything. Did you find it? Where is it?" The whole assembly was silent. "Nobody understands, so I will show you one clear mystic thing. The mystic bird cannot dream on the tree. The mystic flower opens on the tree without shadow or roots."

- Originally there are no six roots, six dusts, or six consciousnesses. Then what?
- What is the meaning of the mystic bird?
- What is the meaning of the mystic flower?

COMMENTARY

The bear catches the bird and laughs, "Ha, ha, ha!"

195

Attaining Don't-Know Is Your True Nature

One day Zen Master Ko Bong, seated on a high rostrum, hit his Zen stick on the table three times and composed this poem aloud:

> *If you want to understand,*
> *You don't understand.*
> *If you attain don't-know,*
> *That is your true nature.*

Then he said, "The Buddha sat under the Bodhi tree for si[x] years, only don't-know. Bodhidharma sat in Sorim for nine years, also don't-know. If you want to understand something, you will go to hell like an arrow. If you attain don't-know you will get the Buddha's head and Bodhidharma's body. Even if you have a lot of money, a high position, many academic degrees, and great power, none of them can help your true self. If you take a rotten rope and tie it to a cloud, that will help your life a little bit. If you can put the whole world into a mustard seed, then you can understand your true nature. But at that time, what do you see, what do you hear? If you see or hear something you will go to hell. And if you cannot see or near something you will lose your body. What can you do?"

Then, holding up the Zen stick, he hit the table and said:

North Mountain, white hair.

South stream, water flowing—DOL, DOL, DOL.

1 ⊘ "If you attain don't-know, that is your true nature."
What does that mean?

2 ⊘ The Buddha sat under the Bodhi tree for six years.
Bodhidharma sat in Sorim for nine years. What did
they get?

3 ⊘ If you see or hear something you will go to hell. And if
you cannot hear something you will lose your body.
What can you do?

4 ⊘ "North mountain, white hair. South stream, water
flowing—DOL, DOL, DOL." What does that mean?

COMMENTARY

Watch out! Big thief!!

25 O'clock

Sitting on the high rostrum, Zen Master Ko Bong hit his Zen stick three times and said, "The Buddha and all the eminent teachers don't understand this point and cannot give transmission of this point. If you go one step forward, you die; if you go one step backward, you die. Also, you cannot stay at this point. Nobody can help you. You can neither open your mouth nor move your body.

"How do you stay alive? If you stay alive, you are the same as the Buddha and all the eminent teachers, but you lose one leg and one eye. So where do you find one leg and one eye? Only go straight don't-know. If you pass 25 o'clock, you can find one leg and one eye. So how do you pass 25 o'clock?"

He held up the Zen stick, then hit the table three times and said, "Be careful! Be careful!!"

1. Zen Master Ko Bong hit the table three times. Why can't the Buddha and all the eminent teachers attain this point?

2. You cannot do anything. How do you stay alive?

3. How do you pass 25 o'clock?

4. "Be careful! Be careful!!" What does this mean?

Swallowed the ten directions, but still hungry.

"KAN!"

Zen Master Ko Bong, sitting on a high rostrum, hit his Zen stick three times and said, "All great Zen Masters teach the whole world about one point. But this one point cannot be seen or heard, and it has no name and no form, so opening their mouths is already a big mistake. How can you make these great Zen Masters' teaching correct? If you want to do that, don't check good and bad, don't hold life and death, and put down your opinion and condition. Only go straight through the raging fires and attain no form, no emptiness. Then you will wake up to the wooden chicken's crowing."

Holding up his stick, he asked, "Do you see?" Then, hitting it on the table, "Do you hear?" He paused for a second, and then asked, "Did you find your original face? How many eyes are there?"

After a moment of silence he shouted, "KATZ!"

Then he said, "KAN!" ("Look!")

All the Zen Masters teach one point, but that one

point is nothing. How do you teach nothing?

2 How do you get through the raging fire?

3 Did you hear the wooden chicken crowing?

4 What does "KAN!" mean?

COMMENTARY

If you open your mouth, you go to hell like an arrow. Close your mouth, you lose your life. What do you see now, what do you hear now? Just do it.

"MYUNG! MYUNG!"

One day Zen Master Ko Bong said from the high rostrum, "If you have no Dharma, you have no demon, but you fall into emptiness. If you are attached to emptiness, even the Buddha and Bodhidharma cannot save you. So it is important to make your Dharma very strong.

"How can you kill your demon? If you are a strong student your weapons are Great Faith, Great Courage, and Great Question. But where do Great Faith, Great Courage, and Great Question come from?

"If you make something, you cannot use these three weapons. If you don't make anything, you still cannot use them. What can you do? If you open your mouth, you go to hell. If you close your mouth, you are a rockhead. Do you understand that? I am giving you good medicine which will make all your sickness disappear. Then everything is complete."

Holding up his Zen stick and hitting the table, he said, "MYUNG! MYUNG!" ("Clear!")

1. ◎ Dharma and demon, which one do you like?
2. ◎ How do you kill your demon?
3. ◎ How do you find Great Faith, Great Courage, and Great Question?
4. ◎ "MYUNG! MYUNG!" What does it mean?

COMMENTARY

The Buddha sat under the Bodhi tree for six years. Bodhidharma sat in Sorim for nine years. If you attain the true meaning of this, be careful about opening your mouth.

Zen Master Hahn Am's KATZ and Hit

Zen Master Hahn Am sat on the high rostrum in silence. He held up the Zen stick and hit the rostrum three times, and then shouted "KATZ!" three times. "If you find the Buddha's and eminent teachers corpses in 'KATZ' and Hit, your original face already appears clearly," he said to the assembly. "If you cannot, you go to hell like an arrow."

1. ⊘ Silence, Hit, KATZ: are they the same or different?
2. ⊘ Can you find your original face in KATZ or Hit?
3. ⊘ What is the meaning of "Go to hell like an arrow"?

Commentary

Hahn Am never got out of hell. The Zen stick has already saved all beings.

Cloud Appears Over South Mountain

Zen Master Kyong Ho asked Zen Master Hahn Am, "Somebody hears 'Cloud appears over South Mountain, rain over North Mountain' and gets enlightenment. What do they attain?"

Zen Master Hahn Am replied, "In front of the meditation

room there are many roof tiles."

1  "Cloud appears over South Mountain, rain over North Mountain."" What does that mean?

2 Is Zen Master Hahn Am's answer correct or not?

COMMENTARY

If you see something, you become blind. If you hear something, you become deaf. If you open your mouth, you become mute. Without making anything, you already find a good answer.

YOU DON'T KNOW. HOW CAN I TEACH YOU?

During the Japanese occupation of Korea, a Japanese Soto Zen Master visited Zen Master Hahn Am and asked, "What is Buddhism's true meaning?"

Hahn Am held up his glasses. Then the Japanese Zen Master said, "You are a great Zen Master. You have studied many sutras and meditated for many years. What did you attain?"

Hahn Am said, "You must go to the Palace of Silence and Stillness and bow."

Then the Japanese Zen Master asked, "You came to this

temple in your youth and became a monk. You have stayed here for forty years. Your mind before coming here and your mind now—are they the same or different?"

Hahn Am replied, "You don't know. How can I teach you?"

1. ☉ What is Buddhism's true meaning?
2. ☉ If you were Zen Master Hahn Am, what could you say you attained?
3. ☉ What is the meaning of "You don't know. How can I teach you"?

COMMENTARY

Two wrestling bears hit the rocks and fall down.

Hyo Bong's Enlightenment

Before Hyo Bong Sunim became a monk and ultimately a great Zen Master, he was a judge during the Japanese occupation of Korea. One day, the police brought a member of the Korean resistance movement before him. According to laws imposed by the Japanese, anyone convicted of resistance activities would be put to death. "What shall I do?" Hyo Bong thought. "If I act correctly as a judge, this man must die, but if I love my country, I cannot punish him." He became very confused, and could not do anything, so he resigned his position and devoted himself to studying the Buddha's teachings. After meeting Zen Master Im Sok Du at Shin Gae Sah Temple on Diamond Mountain, he shaved his head and became a monk.

Hyo Bong practiced very hard, sitting in meditation for hours with unmoving determination. He would never even lie down to sleep. One day a strong wind blowing through the pine trees caused a branch to snap. "Crack!" Upon hearing the sound, Hyo Bong got enlightenment, and composed the following poem:

> *Under the sea is a dove's house. The dove is holding a deer's egg.*
> *In the fire-spider's house they're making fish tea.*
> *Who understands the family tradition?*
> *White cloud flies west, the moon running east.*

1. What is the meaning of the first and second lines?
2. What is the meaning of "White cloud flies west, the moon running east"?

COMMENTARY

Wonderful, wonderful! A great man catches a cloud, turns it into a horse and flies into the sky.

A Gate

Zen Master Hyo Bong gave a Dharma speech in which he said: "There is a gate. From the East, this gate looks like the West Gate. From the West, this gate looks like the East Gate. From the South, it looks like the North Gate, and from the North, it looks like the South Gate. The three worlds of the Buddhas, Bodhisattvas, and eminent teachers are all coming and going through this gate. How do you go through this gate?"

Holding his stick for a moment in silence, he hit the table and said, "If you come through this gate, I will hit you. If you go through this gate, I will also hit you. What can you do?"

1. ⊘ What is this gate?

2. ⊘ Going or coming, Zen Master Hyo Bong will hit you. How do you pass this gate?

Commentary

Don't make anything, don't make anything. If you open your mouth, you have already passed through the gate to hell.

Bodhidharma's Family Tradition

During a Dharma speech, Zen Master Hyo Bong posed a kong-an to the assembly: "Three men are walking. The first man says, 'I am coming here just like this.' The third man says, 'Put it all down.'

"Which one is correct? If you find this, I will hit you thirty times. If you cannot find this, I will also hit you thirty times. What can you do?" Nobody could answer. Then he made a poem:

> *Write "Mu" in the sky —*
> *There is substance and great function.*
> *Meditation and enlightenment are important.*
> *But you must find Bodhidharma's family tradition.*

He then hit the table three times with his Zen stick and descended from the high stand.

1. ⊘ Of the three men, which one is correct?
2. ⊘ How do you write "Mu" in the sky?
3. ⊘ What are "substance and great function"?
4. ⊘ What is Bodhidharma's family tradition?

COMMENTARY

In the sky, one sun, one moon, and many stars. But the blind man cannot see the sun, the moon, or the stars.

205

Where Is the True Master?

Zen Master Hyo Bong once said to a group of students: "Front and back, right and left, everywhere is the true master. If you look for the true master, you will never find it, and you will never get out of the ocean of suffering. But I have a ship with no bottom. Everybody board this ship, and then you can get out of this ocean. All aboard! Hurry up, hurry up!"

Hitting the table with his Zen stick, Hyo Bong recited this poem:

> One step, two steps, three steps.
> Don't check around—only go straight.
> When water and mountain disappear.
> Your original home already appears.

1. Your true master is everywhere. Do you see? Do you hear?
2. How do you ride the ship with no bottom?
3. What is the meaning of "When water and mountains disappear, your original home already appears?"

Commentary

Wake up from your dream! What do you see now? What do you hear now? The mountain is blue, the water is flowing.

Deceiving All Buddhas and Eminent Teachers

One day, Zen Master Hyo Bong delivered a Dharma speech from the high rostrum. "If you open your mouth, you deceive all Buddhas and eminent teachers. If you don't open your mouth, you deceive the whole assembly. How do you not deceive all Buddhas, eminent teachers and the assembly?"

Zen Master In Gak stood up and called out, "Attendant! One cup of tea for the Zen Master."

Then Hyo Bong said, "That's OK, but why didn't you pull me from the high stand?? Today's Dharma speech is already finished, but somebody doesn't have enough mind, so I will make a poem for him:

> *I look at this world.*
> *Nobody escapes life and death.*
> *If you want to take away your suffering,*
> *Throw life, death, and Nirvana into the garbage.*"

1. How do you not deceive all Buddhas, eminent teachers, and the assembly?

2. If at that time somebody appeared and pulled Zen Master Hyo Bong from the high stand, and if you were Hyo Bong, what could you do?

3 How do you throw life, death, and Nirvana into the garbage?

COMMENTARY

There are many stars in the sky, and many trees on the mountain. Birds sing in the trees. See clearly, hear clearly. Everything is complete. Silence is better than holiness.

207

Live Words and Dead Words

During a Dharma speech, Zen Master Hyo Bong said, "In our practice there are live words and dead words. If you attain live words, you are the same as the Buddha and eminent teachers. If you are attached to dead words, you never get out of the ocean of suffering. Live words and dead words are the same as dust in your eyes. So I ask you, how do you get the dust out of your eyes? Tell me! Tell me!" Hyo Bong was silent for a few moments, and then hit his Zen stick on the table three times and descended from the high stand.

1 Live words and dead words: are they the same or different?

2 How do you get the dust out of your eyes?

3   Which are live words: silence or three hits of the Zen stick?

COMMENTARY

Who can save Hyo Bong? If you want to save him, you must use a hammer with handle

Appearing and Disappearing

Zen Master Hyo Bong once said, "Everything is appearing and disappearing. But everything comes from complete stillness. This stillness is substance. If you attain substance, you attain truth and correct function. Then appearing and disappearing are truth, and the correct function of appearing and disappearing is possible.

"My question to all of you is, where do substance, truth, and function come from? If you open your mouth, you already make opposites. If you close your mouth, you are attached to emptiness. How do you, with your mouth not open and not closed, attain substance, truth, and function?"

Nobody could answer.

"I'll give you a hint," he continued. "KATZ! Everybody return to your rooms and drink tea."

1 🕙 Are appearing, disappearing, and stillness the same or different?

2 🕙 What is substance? What is truth? What is function?

3 🕙 What is the meaning of "KATZ!" and "Return to your rooms and drink tea"?

COMMENTARY

Aigo, aigo, aigo! Where do you find Hyo Bong's original body? Watch your step!

ZEN MASTER HYO BONG'S THREE GATES

First Gate: There is an animal on Maitreya Mountain which has the body of a dog and the head of a tiger. What do you call it? Is it a tiger or a dog?

Second Gate: There is a dark moon and a white moon in the sky. The dark moon is going from west to east. The white moon is going from east to west. The two moons come together and become one. What does this mean?

Third Gate: The whole world is a furnace. How did part of it get to be snow?

209

Commentary

One action is better than ten thousand words.

Ten Mu Sicknesses

Zen Master Yong Song received a visit from Zen Master Ko Am, and asked his guest, "In Joju's Mu kong-an there are ten kinds of sickness. How do you not get sick?"

"I'm only walking on the edge of the sword," Ko Am replied.

📿 What are the ten Mu sicknesses?

📿 "Walking on the edge of the sword." What does this mean?

Commentary

Go ask a cow. You will get a beautiful answer.

Lion's Den

Zen Master Yong Song asked Zen Master Ko Am, "What is the meaning of the Buddha's picking up a flower and showing it to Mahakashyapa?"

Zen Master Ko Am answered, "In the lion's den there are no other animals."

1 ◔ What is the meaning of the Buddha's picking up a flower and showing it to Mahakashyapa?

2 ◔ Why are there no other animals in the lion's den?

Commentary

Mistake, mistake, mistake. If you attain the Buddha's mistake, you will attain the Buddha's flower.

The Sky Is High, the Ground Is Thick

212

Zen Master Yong Song once asked Zen Master Ko Am, "The Sixth Patriarch said, 'The flag is not moving, the wind is not moving. Your mind is moving.' What does this mean?"

Zen Master Ko Am stood up, bowed three times, and answered, "The sky is high, the ground is thick."

1 ◔ If you were Zen Master Ko Am, how would you answer?

2 ◔ What is the meaning of "The sky is high, the ground is thick"?

COMMENTARY

Hear a sound, fall down. See something, lose your life.

213

Dharma Transmission

Ko Am asked Zen Master Yong Song, "What is your family teaching tradition?"

Zen Master Yong Song, holding a Zen stick, hit the table three times and said, "What is your family teaching tradition?" Ko Am took the stick and hit the table three times. Then Yong Song said, "Moonlight for 10,000 years," and gave him inga and transmission. Then he wrote this poem for Ko Am:

> TRANSMISSION POEM
>
> *The Buddha and eminent teachers originally don't know;*
> *Shaking my head, I also don't know.*
> *Un Mun's cake is round.*
> *Chinju's mu* is long.*

1. Are Zen Master Yong Song's tradition and Zen Master Ko Am's tradition the same or different?

2. What is the meaning of "Moonlight for 10,000 years"?

* Mu means "radish."

3 ⊘ How big is Un Mun's cake?

4 ⊘ How long is Chinju's mu?

COMMENTARY

Yong Song and Ko Am hug each other and fall down into an old well.

What Is One Thing?

Zen Master Yong Song once gave a Dharma speech, in which he said, "Everyone has one thing. This one thing swallowed heaven, earth, and everything. If you want to find it, it's already far away. If you put it down, it's always in front of you. Brighter than the sun and darker than black ink, it always abides under your palm. Have you found it?"

1 ⊘ How did the one thing swallow everything?

2 ⊘ What is the meaning of "If you want to find it, it's already far away. If you put it down, it's always in front of you"?

3 ⊘ What is the meaning of "Brighter than the sun and darker than black ink"?

4 ⊘ Have you found it under your palm?

COMMENTARY

If the Sixth Patriarch were there, he would have hit Yong Song right in the face.

DONG SAHN'S ZEN STICK

215

Holding his Zen stick, Zen Master Dong Sahn said from the high rostrum, "If you say that this is a Zen stick, it will hit you thirty times. If you say that it is not a Zen stick, it will also hit you thirty times. If you can find the original Zen stick's substance, you will go beyond life and death and attain the land of Buddha. How can you, without speech, attain this Zen stick's substance?"

Then, hitting the table with his stick, he said, "Hit the leg of Blue Mountain, then pick up the East Ocean's head."

1 ⊙ How do you attain the Zen stick's substance?

2 ⊙ How do you attain the land of Buddha?

3 ⊙ "Hit the leg of Blue Mountain, then pick up the East Ocean's head." What does that mean?

Correct action is better than the Buddha's speech.

DRAGON TRACKS

Zen Master Dong Sahn, sitting on the high rostrum, hit his Zen stick three times and said, "Human beings are coming and going on a bridge. This bridge is flowing, while the water underneath is not flowing. An eminent teacher once said, 'when there is no dream, no thinking, and no action, where is your true master?'"

After a moment of silence he continued, "Everybody at this moment has attained their true self. Coming and going, you are completely free. But there is still a single hair on your head. How can you take away that single hair?"

Holding up the Zen stick, then hitting the table, he said, "Sitting, cut off all thinking and look in the ten directions. There you will see dragon tracks."

1 "Human beings are coming and going on a bridge. This bridge is flowing while the water underneath is not flowing." What does this mean?

2 🕮 No dream, no thinking, no action. Where is your true master?

3 🕮 How do you take away one single hair?

4 🕮 How do you find dragon tracks in the ten directions?

COMMENTARY

Open your mouth, lose your tongue. Close your mouth, lose your life. What are you doing just now? Just do it!

"GAM" and "EEE"

217

Zen Master Dong Sahn, hitting the table with his Zen stick, said, "Leaves from a maple tree fell down a deep well, and heaven and earth appeared. A long time ago Zen Master Un Mun, sitting on a high rostrum, looked at the assembly and shouted, 'GAM!' ("gam" means look.) A monk stood up to ask a question of Un Mun, but right at that moment the Zen Master shouted, 'EEE!' ("eee" means sad.) If you attain those two sounds, 'GAM!' and 'EEE!,' you attain live Zen. If you don't understand those two words, you only have dead Zen."

Then Dong Sahn asked, "What are Un Mun's 'GAM' and

'EEE?' Are they the same or different?"

Everybody was silent, so Dong Sahn composed a poem:

> *Looking at each other, not moving an eyelash:*
> *You are east, I am west.*
> *Western dawn across the ocean,*
> *Bright sun through Sumi Mountain.*

1. ◎ Where are the leaves of the maple tree?
2. ◎ What do the Zen Master's "GAM" and "EEE" mean?
3. ◎ What is live Zen and what is dead Zen?
4. ◎ How does the sun get through Sumi Mountain?

COMMENTARY

Don't make anything. See and hear clearly. The moon rises in the West, the sun sets in the West.

The Stone Lion's Roar

One of the most famous monks in all of Thailand visited Zen Master Dong Sahn. The great Korean Zen Master warmly received his guest, saying, "When I went to your country, you gave me many beautiful presents and did many kind

218

deeds for me, so today I would like to give you a present." He then pointed to a stone lion and said, "Do you see this lion?"

"Yes."

"Do you hear the lion's roar?"

The monk was completely dumbfounded, and could not answer.

Zen Master Dong Sahn said, "That is my present to you."

1 ⊙ Do you hear the stone lion's roar?

2 ⊙ What was Zen Master Dong Sahn's present to the monk from Thailand?

COMMENTARY

Don't tell your dream to a rockhead.

MOON Guest

219

Once a monk asked Zen Master Gum Oh, "What is Buddha?"

"There is a bright moon in the sky and guests are coming."

1 ⊙ "There is a bright moon in the sky and guests are coming." What does that mean?

2 ⊙ If you were the monk, what could you say to this?

Kong-Ans

The Sixth Patriarch said, "Originally nothing." If you make something, you lose your life.

If You Want to Meet the Buddha

Zen Master Gum Oh told a group of his students, "Everybody understands where the Buddha's house is. It's called the Palace of Stillness and Extinction. The Palace columns are made of rabbit's horn, and the roof of turtle's hair. If you find this palace and open the door, you will meet the true Buddha."

1 ◌ Where is the Palace of Stillness and Extinction?
2 ◌ How do you make rabbit's horn columns and a turtle's hair roof?
3 ◌ How do you open the door of the palace and meet the true Buddha?

COMMENTARY

If you have ears, you lose your life. If you have no ears, you are better than the Buddha.

Dharma Without Eyes, Ears, or Mouth

Zen Master Gum Oh once said, "If you see something, you are blind. If you hear something, you are deaf. If you open your mouth, you are dumb. So how can you teach the Dharma to all beings?"

What is the meaning of:

1. ☉ "If you see something, you are blind."
2. ☉ "If you hear something, you are deaf."
3. ☉ "If you open your mouth, you are dumb."
4. ☉ No eyes, no ears, no mouth: How do you help all beings?

COMMENTARY

Look, look! Big thief! No mind, no problem. If you have mind, it is already stolen.

Oriole and Stork

Zen Master Jun Kang composed a poem aloud:

An oriole sitting in the tree
becomes a flower.
A stork standing in the garden
becomes a patch of snow.

Then he said, "That is Buddha's mind. But if you attain Buddha from the poem, you will lose your body. If you don't attain Buddha from this poem, this stick will hit you thirty times. What can you do?

After a moment of silence he said, "Already appeared."

1. ☺ Did you find Buddha in this poem?
2. ☺ "If you attain Buddha from this poem, you will lose your body." Why?
3. ☺ After a moment he said, "Already appeared." What does this mean?

COMMENTARY

Originally no words, no body, no Buddha. Big mistake! Go drink tea.

No Nostrils

223

Sitting on the high rostrum before a large assembly of monks, Zen Master Jun Kang hit his Zen stick three times and said, "When our grandteacher Zen Master Kyong Ho got enlightenment he wrote a poem:

When I hear somebody say 'no nostrils,'
I know three thousand worlds are my home.
Yong Nam Mountain in June—
A free man makes a peace song.

"The first and second lines are very good, but the last line has a mistake. If you find this mistake, you attain Zen Master Kyong Ho's mind. If you cannot find the mistake, you are a blind dog."

1. What did Zen Master Kyong Ho attain?
2. Jun Kang said that the last line has a mistake. Where is it?
3. Zen Master Jun Kang said, "If you find the mistake, you attain Zen Master Kyong Ho's mind." What does this mean?

COMMENTARY

The clever man sees a rope and makes a snake out of it. The stupid man sees a rock and bows.

HANGING ON a VINE

Zen Master Yong Sahn sent this story to all the Zen Masters in Korea, and asked them to write back with a response:

224

"A man was being chased by a wild elephant across a field. He stumbled into an old well, and as he was falling, grabbed hold of a vine which was hanging from the inside of the well. He looked down and saw three poisonous snakes at the bottom of the well, while above, the elephant was still waiting for him. A black mouse and a white mouse began gnawing on the vine just as honey from a plant growing on the side of the well began dripping into his mouth. If you were this man, how could you stay alive?"

Each Zen Master sent a reply:

Man Gong: "Last night I had a dream, so I woke up."

Hae Wol: "If you want to understand, you cannot understand. Only don't-know."

Hae Bong: "Buddha cannot see Buddha."

Yong Sahn: "Flower falls down, flax in the garden."

Bo Wol: "How do you fall into the well?"

Jun Kang: "Sweet!"

Ko Bong and Hyong Gak both wrote: "Aigo, aigo!"

Chung Soeng: Only laughing.

Hae Am: "Already dead."

Tan Ho: "Water flowing, never stopping."

1  If you were there at that time, how could you stay alive?

2 Which one is the best answer?

COMMENTARY

Be careful. Open your mouth, already a big mistake.
Thinking, you lose your life. Just do it.

Half a Mu

225

One morning, Zen Master Jun Kang visited Zen Master
Hae Bong at Mah Gok Sah Temple and said to him, "I don't
like Joju's 'Mu.' I like half a 'Mu.' Please give me half a 'Mu.'"

Hae Bong said, "Mu!"

"That's not half a 'Mu.'"

"Then what is half a 'Mu?'"

Jun Kang said, "Mu!"

Laughing hard, Hae Bong said, "You are very clever."

1 Joju said "Mu," and that is a big mistake. Where is
Joju's mistake?

2 If somebody asks you to give half a "Mu," what can
you say?

COMMENTARY

Two mud cows, wrestling, fall into the ocean. Which one
wins, which one loses? No news.

Originally Nothing

When Zen Master Jun Kang visited Zen Master Hae Am
at the Diamond Mountain Ji Jang Bosal Temple, Hae Am
asked him, "The Sixth Patriarch wrote 'Originally nothing,'
and then got transmission. What did he get?" Jun Kang only
clapped his hands three times.

1 ⟳ What does "Originally nothing" mean?
2 ⟳ Is Jun Kang's answer correct or not?

COMMENTARY

Mistake, mistake, mistake. A second offense is not permitted. You must ask the stone girl.

227

First Word

Zen Master Jun Kang visited Zen Master Yong Song and was asked, "What is the first word?"

"Yes!"

"No!" Yong Song replied.

Jun Kung clapped his hands and laughed.

Yong Song again said, "No!"

"I ask you then, what is the first word?"

"Jun Kang!"

"Yes!" Jun Kang replied.

"That is the first word," Yong Song said.

1. What is the first word?
2. What is the last word?

COMMENTARY

If you open your mouth, the first word and the last word both appear. If you close your mouth, they both disappear. Without any mouth, the first and last word are already clear.

Hair Grows on Wide Teeth

Zen Master Jun Kang always posed the following kong-an to his students: "A long time ago, someone asked Zen Master Joju, 'Why did Bodhidharma come to China?' Joju replied, 'Hair grows on wide teeth.' If you attain this you can see Bodhidharma's true face. If you don't understand this, you don't know Joju or Bodhidharma."

1 ⊘ "Hair grows on wide teeth." What does that mean?

2 ⊘ What is Bodhidharma's true face?

3 ⊘ "If you don't understand this, you don't know Joju or Bodhidharma." What does this mean?

Commentary

The snake's beard grows for a thousand miles. The rabbit's horn grows and pierces the moon.

Thorny Jungle Everywhere

Zen Master Jun Kang gave a Dharma speech from the high rostrum, saying, "Upon his enlightenment, Zen Master Man Gong composed this poem:

Empty mountain, true energy without time and space.
White cloud and clear wind come and go by themselves.
Why did Bodhidharma come to China?
Rooster crowing in the morning,
Sun rising in the east.

Then Jun Kang said, "If you attain this poem, you attain the meaning of all the sutras. The last two lines are the most important: 'Rooster crowing in the morning, Sun rising in the east.'"

"If you find that point, then you find Bodhidharma's heart and the Buddha's head. So I ask you, where is Bodhidharma's heart and Buddha's head?"

After holding up the Zen stick in silence for a moment, he shouted, "KATZ!"

Then he said, "Thorny jungle everywhere."

1 ◎ What did you attain from Zen Master Man Gong's poem?
2 ◎ Zen Master Jun Kang said, "If you find that point, you find Bodhidharma's heart and Buddha's head." What does this mean?
3 ◎ "Thorny jungle everywhere." What does this mean?
4 ◎ How do you get out of this thorny jungle?

COMMENTARY

Look, look! Big thief! Watch your pockets.

TRUE EMPTINESS

Zen Master Jun Kang visited Zen Master Hae Wol, and was asked, "What does true emptiness and stillness mystic wisdom mean?"

Jun Kang replied, "Cannot hear, cannot see."

"No," Hae Wol said.

"Cannot hear, cannot see!"

But Hae Wol said, "Big mistake!"

1 ⊘ What is emptiness and stillness mystic wisdom?

2 ⊘ Where is Jun Kang's mistake?

COMMENTARY

Two stone girls face each other. Together they laugh, "Ha, ha, ha!"

Zen

Ma Jo's Circle

One day, Zen Master Bo Wol asked Zen Master Jun Kang, "A long time ago, Zen Master Ma Jo said to the assembly, 'I have a circle. If you enter this circle, I will hit you. If you do not enter this circle, I will also hit you. What can you do?' So I ask you, Jun Kang, if you had been there, how would you have answered?"

Jun Kang replied, "I don't like nonsense. How do you not get hit by Ma Jo's stick?"

Bo Wol answered, "Why are you holding Ma Jo's stick?"

1. If you had been there, how would you have answered Ma Jo's question?

2. Where is Jun Kang's mistake?

COMMENTARY

Your feet are walking on the ground. Your arms are moving back and forth.

Ko Bong's No Hindrance Person

Many years ago, the Chinese Zen Master Ko Bong said to a group of monks, "There is a person who is made of nothing but skin with holes, rotting flesh, and broken bones, but still this person's speech is no hindrance. How wonderful! This person's actions, coming and going, hit and break all space, and swallow the big ocean.

"If you want to know who this is, you must understand the following: The mud cow eats the steel stick and spits blood on the guardian angel."

1. Nothing but skin with holes, rotting flesh, and broken bones. How do you become a person with no hindrance?
2. How does the person with no hindrance swallow the big ocean?
3. Where is the mud cow?
4. Who is the guardian angel?

COMMENTARY

Blood fills the sky. Bone appears all over the earth. How can you breathe clean air? How do you walk around in the ten directions? Watch your step!

Mistake

Zen Master Kyong Bong, sitting before an assembly, hit his Zen stick on the rostrum and said, "All Buddhas and all eminent teachers made a big mistake, because opening one's mouth is already a mistake. So how do you correct all the Buddhas and eminent teachers? If you make their mistake correct, this stick will hit you thirty times. If you do not make their mistake correct, this stick will also hit you thirty times. What can you do?"

After holding the stick a moment in silence, he said:

> *The geese with no shadows*
> *Fly in cold moonlight.*
> *Stone lion running east,*
> *North star moving west.*

After another moment of silence he shouted, "KATZ!" then commented, "And this is also a big mistake."

1 Where is all Buddhas' and eminent teachers' mistake? What does the Zen Master's poem mean?

2 At the end he said, "And this is also a big mistake." What does this mean?

This stick has already hit Zen Master Kyong Bong thirty times. Aigo, aigo, aigo!

234

WHERE IS YOUR HOMETOWN?

One winter, Zen Master Chun Song stayed at Nang Wol Sah Temple. It was very cold, and there were many students there for Kyol Che, so the Zen Master told the students to cut down some trees for firewood. But there was a law against cutting down trees, so a policeman came and took Chun Song to the police station.

The police asked him, "Why did you cut down the trees?"

"Because it's cold and we have no wood."

"That is illegal! Where is your hometown?"

The Zen Master answered, "My father's X X X."

"WHAT!? Where is your hometown?"

The Zen Master said, "I already told you—my father's X X X."

The policeman yelled, "Are you crazy?"

"No," said the Zen Master.

"Where do you come from?" asked the policeman.

"From my mother's X X X."

"WHAT!?"

"I already said, from my mother's X X X."

"You're crazy!!" the policeman shouted. "Go away!" And so Zen Master Chun Song was released.

1 Ⓩ Why did Chun Song cut down the trees?

2 Ⓩ Is this Zen Master crazy, or is he a Bodhisattva?

COMMENTARY

The crying boy wants candy. The old woman likes donuts.

One Pure and Clear Thing

One day Zen Master Man Gong gave a Dharma speech in which he said, "Even if this world explodes, if everyone has one pure and clear thing, it will never disappear. That thing sometimes dreams, sometimes is awake. Then I ask you, not-dreaming and not-awake, where is it?"

1 Ⓩ When everything explodes, where is the one pure and clear thing?

2 During not-dreaming time and not-awake time, where does it stay?

COMMENTARY

When you are hungry, go to the kitchen. When you are tired, go to the bedroom.